ParalympicsGB

The true story of Great Britain's

Paralympic
Heroes

First published by Carlton Books Limited in 2011
Copyright © 2011 Carlton Books Limited

Carlton Books Limited
20 Mortimer Street
London, W1T 3JW

ParalympicsGB Lion's head logo TM © BPA 2005–2010

A CIP catalogue record for this book is available from the British Library.

ISBN: 978-1-84732-811-3

Printed in Great Britain by CPI Mackays, Chatham ME5 8TD

ParalympicsGB

The true story of Great Britain's

Paralympic Heroes

Cathy Wood

Introduction by **Chris Holmes, MBE**
Foreword by **Ellie Simmonds, MBE**

CARLTON

For Beryl

Contents

Introduction

It's 4.40am and my alarm clock rudely rings in another day as it has done for the past 11 years and, unknown to me, will continue to do so for the coming six. The year is 1996 and I'm in the final stages of training for the Atlanta 1996 Paralympic Games. It's a freezing February morning and my gold medal hopes, never mind the proverbial wild horses, aren't enough to drag me from my quilted cocoon. What gets me out of bed, as ever, is the thought of the other 18 City of Birmingham swimmers I train with who are all feeling the same, knowing it is their job to be there, to ensure we work out as one, to move forward as a group, as a team.

So what does it take to be a Paralympian? The true magic of the Paralympic Games is that there is no magic. Instead, perfect planning, complete commitment, unfailing teamwork and, for me, literally thousands of hours and millions of metres in the swimming pool is what converted into gold. Knowing what you are doing and why, with every session planned and every decision resting on the answer to one question – will it improve my race time? And if the answer is not in the affirmative, why am I doing it?

The glorious Paralympic Games are at their best when competition takes part in front of buzzing crowds, as was the case at Barcelona 1992. A packed Aquatics Centre was bathed in Spanish sunshine and, for me, marked the culmination of seven years of hard yards. To have the luck, the fantastic fortune, to win six gold medals at a single Games proved the power of the team – not individual achievement, but shared success. Four years later, I defended my titles at Atlanta 1996 then went on to compete at Sydney 2000. In all, this blessed me with nine gold medals from three Paralympic Games, friendships from East to West and memories etched forever in my heart and mind.

Now, sitting in my office, a mere ball throw away from the Olympic Park where the action will take place at London 2012, I reflect on my Paralympic Games past and consider the future for the Games. We have many goals for London 2012 including stadiums full of excited fans, millions of viewers across the country tuning in and billions around the world doing the same, many of whom will be experiencing Paralympic sport for the first time. Channel 4, our domestic broadcast partner, promises more hours of coverage when the Games start than ever before, but even more significantly, complete commitment to promoting Paralympians, Paralympic sport and the Games as a whole, ever since they got involved at the start of 2010. Similarly, the sponsorship provided by Sainsbury's has the potential not just to shift perceptions, but to blast the Paralympic Games into the mainstream. With over 21 million customers going through Sainsbury's stores every week, this means millions of people can get behind our ParalympicsGB team.

And all from such small acorns. Picture Stoke Mandeville Hospital, famous for its treatment of spinal injuries, back in 1948 with a handful of archers on the lawns, competing among each other as part of their rehabilitation. This is where the Paralympic Games were born. Time's arrow has flown, blowing the winds of change through Rome 1960 (the first time both Olympic and Paralympic Games took place in the same city), Seoul 1988 (to many, the first truly modern Paralympic Games), Sydney 2000 (simply superb) and Beijing 2008 (where the Paralympic

Games took on the same splendour as the Olympic Games). Now attention turns to London 2012, where over 4,000 athletes across 20 sports will compete in front of two million spectators in the stadiums and billions more across the globe on television. Our aim for the athletes is simple: to put them at the heart of everything we do and to take care of the detail, so all they have to focus on is pulling out the performance of their lives.

The potential of the Paralympic Games is immense. We aim for a Games that is value-rich and courageous, which seeks to connect and to draw in more than stand out. It has the power to change us as individuals, communities and a country for the better.

And the future? As the Winter and Summer Games go forward to Socci 2014 and Rio 2016 and beyond, their development will surely continue with increased commercial and public interest, more countries competing and more Paralympians transformed into household names and heroes.

Any more than this will inevitably be speculative. What is clear, though, is that the Paralympic Games is coming to London and we all have an extraordinary opportunity to be part of it.

Chris Holmes, MBE, London 2011

Foreword

The Paralympic Games is now one of the world's biggest sporting events and I'm proud to have been part of the British Swimming team at Beijing 2008, an experience that will live with me forever.

There's so much to be in awe of when looking back over the history of the Games and the British athletes who have always done so well. It's an honour to feel that I'm adding to that history, since in many ways I'm just starting out on my own career.

I was so excited at being selected for Beijing 2008 because I didn't think they would take me because of my age – I was 13 at the time. But I couldn't have made it without several key components being in place. The support of my family and coaches was critical, but also the inspiration I get from being part of the Paralympic movement is also very important.

When I reflect on my own career to date I can see how important that support has been. I was invited onto British Swimming's talent programme just after my tenth birthday after taking part in my first disability competition at the age of nine. Everyone on the programme was nurtured and this made us all feel that we might have some ability.

My own role models spurred me on as well. I was inspired by watching Nyree Lewis winning the 100m Backstroke at the Athens 2004 Paralympic Games and she and others, such as Erin Popovich and Michael Phelps, have been my inspiration, all amazing athletes, regardless of whether they compete in the Olympic or Paralympic Games. The feeling of having a gold medal hung around your neck as you stand on the top of the podium is incredible. I was so happy and emotional that it all now seems a blur.

So the Paralympic Games are about striving to see what we're all capable of achieving but there is more to it than just that. The Games are also about community and I have loved the fact that I have made loads of friends at events across the world, both disabled and non-disabled. There is a wonderfully supportive atmosphere among all the swimmers: we are highly competitive in the water on race day, but the best of friends once the racing is over – win or lose – and I love the atmosphere and camaraderie of competitions.

Winning is a great feeling but it is also very important that people, particularly young disabled people, can see that you can achieve your dreams if you really want to and work hard enough. The Paralympic movement has allowed me to achieve my dream, by creating the platform whereby I can compete against others with a similar disability.

So this book about British Paralympic success is close to my heart. It shows how the Games and the athletes have moved on since its conception in 1948, when disabled sport was seen as rehabilitation, to today, where competitors are full-time athletes with the same training regimes as their non-disabled counterparts. Some athletes are now also competing at the top levels of non-disabled sport and it happily seems that the Paralympic Games are fulfilling their vision of being the 'parallel' Games.

Many of the athletes you will come across on the pages of this book have had similar experiences, thoughts and feelings to mine and I hope you enjoy reading about them as a new opportunity for more success comes around at London 2012.

Ellie Simmonds, MBE, Swansea, 2011

ParalympicsGB

The true story of Great Britain's

Paralympic
Heroes

For the Record

The Paralympic Games

From 1948–59, sports competitions for the disabled were held annually at Stoke Mandeville Hospital. In 1952, the first international competitors arrived. The ninth competition, in 1960, was held in Rome and this event is considered to be the first Paralympic Games, which has since been held every four years, in the same year as the Olympic Games.

Rome	1960	Seoul	1988
Tokyo	1964	Barcelona	1992
Tel Aviv	1968	Atlanta	1996
Heidelberg	1972	Sydney	2000
Toronto	1976	Athens	2004
Arnhem	1980	Beijing	2008
New York/Stoke Mandeville	1984		

Athletes featured in this book:

Tom Aggar *DOB:* 24/05/84
Sport: Rowing
Record: Beijing 2008, Gold (Single Sculls – ASM1x)

Danielle Brown *DOB:* 10/04/88
Sport: Archery
Record: Beijing 2008, Gold
(Individual Compound – Open)

Tel Byrne *DOB:* 7/06/84
Sport: Cycling
Record: London 2012 Games hopeful

Sophie Christiansen *DOB:* 14/11/87
Sport: Equestrian
Record: Athens 2004, Bronze (Championships Test: Individual – Grade 1a);
Beijing 2008, Gold (Freestyle Test: Individual – Grade 1a,
Team – Open), Silver (Championships Test: Individual – Grade 1a)

Philip Craven *DOB:* 4/07/50
Sports: Athletics, Wheelchair Basketball, Swimming
Record: Heidelberg 1972, Toronto 1976, Arnhem 1980, New York/Stoke
Mandeville 1984, Seoul 1988

Jody Cundy *DOB:* 14/10/78
   Sports: Swimming and Cycling
   Record: Atlanta 1996, Gold (100m Butterfly – S10); Sydney 2000, Gold
            (100m Butterfly – S10, 4 x 100m Freestyle Relay – 34 points), Bronze
            (100m Backstroke – S10); Athens 2004, Bronze (100m Butterfly –
            S10); Beijing 2008, Gold (1km Time Trial LC2, Team Sprint LC1-4
            CP3/4)

Tanni Grey-Thompson *DOB:* 26/07/69
   Sport: Athletics
   Record: Seoul 1988, Bronze (400m 3); Barcelona 1992, Gold (100m, 200m,
            400m, 800m – TW3), Silver (4 x 100m Relay – TW3-4); Atlanta
            1996, Gold (800m – T52), Silver (100m, 200m, 400m – T52);
            Sydney 2000, Gold (100m, 200m, 400m, 800m – T53); Athens 2004,
            Gold (100m, 400m – T53)

Chris Holmes *DOB:* 15/10/71
   Sport: Swimming
   Record: Seoul 1988, Silver (50m Freestyle, 400m Freestyle – B2), Bronze
            (100m Freestyle – B2); Barcelona 1992, Gold (50m Freestyle,
            100m Freestyle, 400m Freestyle, 100m Backstroke, 200m Backstroke,
            200m Individual Medley – B2), Silver (400m Individual Medley –
            B1-2); Atlanta 1996, Gold (50m Freestyle, 100m Freestyle, 100m
            Backstroke – B2), Silver (200m Individual Medley – B2); Sydney
            2000, Silver (4 x 100m Medley Relay – S11-S13)

Darren Kenny *DOB:* 17/03/70
   Sport: Cycling
   Record: Athens 2004, Gold (1km Time Trial Bicycle CP Div 3/4, Individual
            Pursuit Bicycle CP Div 3), Silver (Time Trial Bicycle CP Div 3);
            Beijing 2008, Gold (Individual Road Race LC3-4 CP3, 1km Time
            Trial CP3, Individual Pursuit CP3, Team Sprint LC1-4 CP3/4),
            Silver (Individual Time Trial CP3)

Margaret Maughan *DOB:* 20/06/28
   Sports: Archery, Dartarchery, Lawn Bowls, Swimming
   Record: Rome 1960, Gold (Archery – Women's Columbia Round Open,
            Swimming – 50m Backstroke); Heidelberg 1972, Gold (Dartarchery –
            Women's Pairs Open); Toronto 1976, Silver (Dartarchery – Women's
            Pairs Open, Lawn Bowls – Women's Pairs); Arnhem 1980, Gold (Lawn
            Bowls – Women's Pairs)

Peter Norfolk *DOB:* 13/12/60
   Sport: Wheelchair Tennis
   Record: Athens 2004, Gold (Singles – Quad), Silver (Doubles – Quad);
         Beijing 2008, Gold (Singles – Quad), Bronze (Doubles – Quad)

Josie Pearson *DOB:* 03/01/86
   Sports: Wheelchair Rugby and Athletics
   Record: Beijing 2008 (Wheelchair Rugby)

Lee Pearson *DOB:* 4/02/74
   Sport: Equestrian
   Record: Sydney 2000, Gold (Championships Test – Grade 1a, Freestyle
         Test – Grade 1a, Team – Open); Athens 2004, Gold (Championships
         Test – Grade 1a, Freestyle Test – Grade 1a, Team – Open); Beijing
         2008, Gold (Championships Test – Grade 1b, Freestyle Test –
         Grade 1b, Team – Open)

Helene Raynsford *DOB:* 29/12/79
   Sport: Rowing
   Record: Beijing 2008, Gold (Single Sculls – ASW1x)

Tim Reddish *DOB:* 12/04/57
   Sport: Swimming
   Record: Barcelona 1992, Silver (100m Butterfly – B1-B2), Bronze (100m
         Freestyle – B2); Atlanta 1996, Silver (200m Individual Medley – B1),
         Bronze (100m Freestyle – B1); Sydney 2000, Silver (4 x 100m Medley
         Relay – S11-S13)

Dave Roberts *DOB:* 25/05/80
   Sport: Swimming
   Record: Sydney 2000, Gold (100m Freestyle – S7, 4 x 100m Freestyle Relay –
         34 points, 50m Freestyle – S7), Silver (100m Backstroke – S7, 400m
         Freestyle – S7, 4 x 100m Medley Relay – 34 points); Bronze (4 x 50m
         Freestyle – 20 points); Athens 2004, Gold (100m Freestyle – S7, 400m
         Freestyle – S7, 4 x 100m Freestyle Relay – 34 points, 50m Freestyle
         – S7), Silver (200m Individual Medley – SM7); Beijing 2008, Gold
         (100m Freestyle – S7, 400m Freestyle – S7, 4 x 100m Freestyle Relay –
         34 points, 50m Freestyle – S7)

Ellie Simmonds *DOB:* 11/11/94
   Sport: Swimming
   Record: Beijing 2008, Gold (100m Freestyle, 400m Freestyle – S6)

Sarah Storey *DOB:* 26/10/77
Sports: Swimming and Cycling
Record: Barcelona 1992, Gold (100m Backstroke – S10, 200m Individual
Medley – SM10), Silver (400m Freestyle – S10, 4 x 100m Freestyle
Relay, 4 x 100m Medley Relay – S7-S10), Bronze (100m Freestyle –
S10); Atlanta 1996, Gold (100m Backstroke – S10, 100m Breaststroke
SB10, 200m Individual Medley – SM10), Silver (400m Freestyle
– S10), Bronze (100m Freestyle – S10); Sydney 2000, Silver (100m
Backstroke – S10, 4 x 100m Medley Relay – 34 points); Athens 2004,
Silver (100m Breaststroke – SB9, 200m Individual Medley – SM10),
Bronze (100m Freestyle – S10); Beijing 2008, Gold (Individual Time
Trail, Individual Pursuit LC1-2/CP4)

Clare Strange *DOB:* 18/09/79
Sport: Wheelchair Basketball
Games: Sydney 2000, Athens 2004, Beijing 2008

Caz Walton *DOB:* 01/02/47
Sports: Athletics, Basketball, Fencing, Swimming, Table Tennis
Record: Tokyo 1964, Gold (Athletics – Slalom, Wheelchair Dash); Tel Aviv
1968, Gold (Athletics – 60m Wheelchair, Slalom, Table Tennis –
Doubles), Silver (Swimming – 100m Breaststroke, Table Tennis –
Singles), Bronze (Pentathlon); Heidelberg 1972, Gold (Athletics – 60m,
4 x 40m Wheelchair Relay, Table Tennis – Singles, Fencing – Foil),
Bronze (Pentathlon); Toronto 1976, Bronze (Athletics – 60m, Table
Tennis – Singles, Fencing – Foil); Seoul 1988, Gold (Fencing – Epée
single)

Dave Weir *DOB:* 05/06/79
Sport: Athletics
Record: Beijing 2008, Gold (1500m, 800m – T54), Silver (400m – T54),
Bronze (5000m – T54)

Richard Whitehead *DOB:* 19/07/76
Sports: Ice Sledge Hockey and Athletics
Record: Turin 2006 (Winter Games); London 2012 hopeful

Martine Wright *DOB:* 30/09/72
Sport: Sitting Volleyball
Record: London 2012 hopeful

Chapter One

The Beginning

'Live your beliefs and you can turn the world around.'

Henry David Thoreau, author

As the distinctive British Airways jumbo jet, with its freshly painted gold nose and matching wings, taxied towards the exclusive VIP entrance at London's Heathrow Terminal 5, on the afternoon of Thursday 18 September 2008, life, for some of the athletes onboard, would never be quite the same again.

For 12 incredible days they had been part of a Paralympic Games that had seen the level of athlete performance reach new heights. They had participated in superbly organised events which had been held in breathtaking venues, contributed to peerless sporting moments and been cheered on by thousands of passionate supporters.

They had seen their teammates win gold in nine of the 18 sports Britain was represented in, and enjoyed the fact that their endeavours were covered by an ever-growing contingent of British media.

Back home millions tuned in to BBC television to catch a glimpse of the Closing Ceremony. In the world of elite sport for athletes with a disability, this was something few had experienced before. Better prepared (and funded) than any previous British team, the investment (and interest), had more than paid off.

Chapter One

In Beijing Team ParalympicsGB excelled, racking up a total of 42 gold medals, 29 silver and 31 bronze, to finish second in the medals table behind the sporting might of China.

The eventual haul – 102 medals – was the equivalent of almost one medal for every second team member on the plane home, and far exceeded the pre-Games target of 40 golds.

And one of the most exciting aspects about Beijing was the team's relative youth. More than half, 119 athletes, were attending their first Games, which meant next time round, they would take all that knowledge, experience and expertise to a Games being held on home soil.

For the competitors every gold-winning performance was memorable, but in three sports in particular – Paralympic Cycling (Road and Track), Equestrian and Paralympic Rowing – such was the depth of the squad's success that Britain finished top of the medal table.

The Paralympic cyclists carried on where Olympic champions like Sir Chris Hoy, Victoria Pendleton and Rebecca Romero left off a few weeks earlier, winning 17 golds in total, and 12 more than second-placed USA. Four were won by a single athlete, Darren Kenny, making him one of the most successful Paralympic cyclists of all time.

Kenny had been a talented teenage rider good enough to take part in the Junior Tour of Ireland. But a crash in the event itself, caused a serious neck injury which ended his career at just 18. For the next 12 years Kenny abandoned cycling before taking it up again in 2000, at the age of 30, to lose weight and get fitter. Four years later he burst onto the Paralympic Cycling scene, taking two gold medals and one silver at Athens 2004. At Beijing 2008 he added four more golds, as well as taking a silver to increase his total to six golds and two silvers.

In Paralympic Equestrian, Lee Pearson took three golds to add to his existing six, three each from Sydney 2000 and Athens 2004. He has an incredible 100 per cent gold medal-winning rate for events entered and is the most successful British disabled rider.

On the track, David Weir, one of the best wheelchair athletes in the world and a five-time London Marathon winner, finally won the first of two gold medals, 12 years after competing in his first Paralympic Games as a 17-year-old at Atlanta 1996. Success was particularly sweet for the London-based athlete because a decade earlier, after the Atlanta Games, he quit Paralympic Athletics for good, or so it seemed.

But watching the Sydney 2000 Paralympic Games at home on his television, Weir was reduced to tears as the realisation of what he could have achieved, had he been there, sank in. Before long he was back training. After a build-up to Beijing 2008 hampered by glandular fever, winning not one, but two gold medals was the best feeling in the world.

And there was success for another long-term servant of British Paralympic sport as swimmer Dave Roberts secured four golds in the pool, retaining the titles he'd won at Athens 2004. Roberts' success had added significance, since it took his Paralympic total to 11 gold medals, equalling the number won by Tanni Grey-Thompson (née Grey and now Baroness), Britain's best-known Paralympian athlete.

'That's the one I came here for,' Roberts said afterwards. 'To be equal with Grey-Thompson is unbelievable, it's something I didn't believe would ever happen.'

Roberts, who was born in Pontypridd, Wales, was diagnosed with Cerebral Palsy (CP) at the age of 11 and then advised to swim as a form of physiotherapy to help him stay supple. Some of his rivals today might wish he had stuck to the advice given and only ever indulged in an occasional, feel-good dip. Instead he turned his disability into a formidable asset. Within three years he was swimming for Wales and by the age of 19 for Britain. At 20 he attended to his first Paralympic Games in Sydney whereupon he came home weighed down by seven medals: three gold, three silver and one bronze.

At the age of 28, with an 11 gold medal stash, Roberts might well have called time on his career after Beijing 2008. And had the 2012 Games been awarded to any city other than London, he probably would have. But the lure of a home Games, something that might never come around again in his lifetime, was too good to miss. And at London 2012 Roberts will have the chance to claim an unrivalled 12th gold medal, which would make him Britain's most decorated Paralympic athlete of all time.

In recognition of his achievements, Roberts was selected to carry the flag at the Closing Ceremony. 'It was the biggest honour of my career,' he said, particularly as he'd missed the Opening Ceremony as it came too close to his first race. Despite the nerves – and fear he might trip up in front of the watching world – he fulfilled his duties with immense pride. 'I remember thinking, "I've made it, my life is made up,"' he said before joining other athletes and spectators in a colourful, extravagant celebratory Ceremony, as China said goodbye to the thousands of athletes whose very presence had been a daily reminder of the indomitable power of the human spirit.

Then came a moment of history, lost on all but a few of the 92,000 spectators looking on. During the Closing Ceremony it is Paralympic Games' protocol to pass the flag of the International Paralympic

Committee (IPC) from the city ending its tenure as host to the Paralympic Games to the one beginning its four-year cycle. At Beijing 2008, Sir Philip Craven, the plain-talking Yorkshireman and President of the IPC, waved the flag aloft before passing it to Boris Johnson, Mayor of London, for safe keeping until 2012. It was a moment that perhaps encapsulated the long-held belief that, in 2012, the Paralympic Games really are coming home.

Britain's name will forever be intertwined with the birth of the Paralympic Movement and yet, in more than 50 years, this country has never been the official host. Nearly a quarter of a century earlier, in 1984, Stoke Mandeville jointly hosted the Games with New York, but this was only after previous arrangements to stage some events in Champaign, Illinois fell through. But Britain as outright hosts? Never, until now, that is. Fittingly, Philip Craven is one of the few people involved for long enough to appreciate the significance of the handover moment.

As the Paralympic Flame was extinguished and the night sky returned to normal after a spectacular fireworks finale, there was time for athletes, of all nations, disabilities and backgrounds, to reflect on the extraordinary bonds and friendships made. Many didn't want to leave.

'Beijing was insane,' said Roberts. 'It was bigger, brighter and louder than any Games I have ever been to. So when the Paralympic Flame goes out it's horrible. It's over, it's finished. And it's going to be another four years until it comes round again. The Games aren't normal, so when the Flame goes out it's time to go home. Reality bites.'

Not surprisingly then, many partied long into the Chinese night, hoping the experience would last that bit longer. After all the hard work and dedication, these were the hours to treasure and celebrate. So it was a rather bleary-eyed team that boarded the 11-hour flight home only to discover that as one party ended, another was just beginning. Extra bottles of champagne had already been loaded into the galleys, together with some very British nibbles. And if the team thought being fêted on board was special even that would fade into insignificance when the plane arrived at its final destination.

There to greet them was a welcoming committee like none other, including then Prime Minister Gordon Brown, and friends, family and supporters, who clapped and cheered as they wheeled or walked into the Arrivals Hall, an array of gold, silver and bronze medals clinking round their necks. Against a backdrop of camera flashes and microphones came press questions and requests, interviews and photo calls.

And there was more to come. Towards the end of 2008, ParalympicsGB teamed up with TeamGB for the first-ever joint Olympic and Paralympic victory parade through the streets of London, with 12 special floats travelling past St Paul's Cathedral, down Fleet Street and into the Strand and Trafalgar Square. Thousands turned out to show support. Even for those who had been part of successful British Paralympic teams from previous Games, that late-autumn October parade surpassed anything that had gone before. Lee Pearson called it, 'the best day of my life', better even than the three gold medals he had won at Beijing 2008, and the nine in total from three Olympic Games.

As the months passed, many Paralympians popped up on the nation's television screens, while a select few were named in the Queen's New Year's Honours List. All were invited to a special reception at Buckingham Palace in February 2009 hosted by HM the Queen and the Duke of

Edinburgh and attended by Camilla, Duchess of Cornwall, and Sophie, Countess of Wessex. Some, like young swimmer Ellie Simmonds, who won the nation over with her tearful celebrations after becoming the youngest-ever individual British Paralympic champion aged just 13, were enjoying unprecedented media interest.

For the athletes the growing warmth and recognition towards them as elite sporting athletes with a disability, rather than disabled men and women to be pitied and patronised for their efforts, made all the work, training, sacrifices and pain worthwhile. 'There has been a stereotypical view that taking part is all that counts,' said Josie Pearson, who became the first woman to represent Great Britain in the mixed sport of Wheelchair Rugby in Beijing. 'But people are realising we are elite athletes and we train like any other elite athlete in the world. I don't do this for fun: I want to be an elite athlete.'

Few experienced the new-found recognition more than Dave Roberts. During his five weeks away, at the pre-Games holding camp and then at the Games themselves, he was forced to leave his five-year-old dog, Lulah, in kennels back home near his Cardiff Bay home.

When he finally returned to pick her up, he found it wasn't just the kennel staff and Lulah who eagerly awaited him. The local press were also there, waiting. 'It's Been Ruff Without You' beamed the headline on the front page of the next day's South Wales Echo.

But that wasn't all. After so long away, the fridge in the Roberts' household was bare and so he headed to his local supermarket for the usual 20-minute dash around the aisles. Only this time replenishing the essentials took hours, not helped by a special announcement over the tannoy to alert fellow shoppers of the star in their midst. 'People kept coming up to me and saying, "Thank you for making me smile,'" Roberts recalled.

And so, as 2008 drew to a close, few in the Paralympic Movement could have dreamed of the extraordinary progress made in such a relatively short time, or of the warm welcome athletes would receive from a proud British public.

It was a very different homecoming to the one experienced in 1960 when a British team returned from Italy for what has now become known as the first Paralympic Games.

***

Although many in the British team in Beijing didn't want the Paralympic experience to end, after little sleep and a long flight back it was, at least for another four years, over. For many athletes, elite sport has become a gateway to see and travel the world.

More than half a century earlier it was a love of travelling that propelled Margaret Maughan into a quite unexpected, pioneering Paralympic role.

Born in June 1928 and brought up in Preston, Lancashire, travel was all Margaret wanted to do. In 1949, at the age of 21, she trained to be a teacher and spent the next five years working in education in England. But she yearned for change and new opportunities, and with the opening up of Britain's colonies, what better way to see the world than to take up a post overseas? Her first stop was the West Indies and then a job teaching Home Economics at a secondary school in Jamaica. Then, in 1958, along came an adventure too good to miss – Margaret was offered a posting to Malawi in Africa to help oversee the Government's education programme for women.

Then known as Nyasaland, Malawi was still part of the Commonwealth and jobs didn't come much better, or further afield, than this. It meant Margaret, now 29, would sail first to South Africa, then to Mozambique, from where she would complete the final part of her journey by train. For a young woman looking to see the world it was the perfect start to an edifying adventure.

Margaret could hardly wait but her younger sister, Ruth, wasn't so enthusiastic. As she waved goodbye to Margaret at Waterloo station, she did so with a growing sense of unease, a feeling that something wasn't quite right. 'I just felt very strange,' she later admitted.

Unaware of her sister's misgivings, Margaret set off, arriving in Malawi in the late summer of 1958, where she set up home in the remote village of Lilongwe, now the country's capital. Her job, as Women's Education Officer for the Central Province, was to ensure local schools adhered to the curriculum laid down by the British Government. By day she would travel around the Province ensuring the schools were well run and the rules followed. By night she enjoyed a lively social life in the company of fellow ex-pats, who had a habit of ensuring that whatever they were doing, Margaret was invited along too.

Christmas 1958 came and went, with any feelings of loneliness or homesickness filled by the kindness and invitations of new friends. By February 1959 Margaret was truly settled, loving her African odyssey and the new experiences it was bringing. Whenever she visited a school under her care she would be greeted by the sound of children's voices wafting through the air as they sang traditional African songs to welcome in the new day. 'I still hear that noise of children singing in the distance,' she later said.

Then one February evening, six months into her trip, a man Margaret barely knew offered her a lift to a party they had both been invited to. With so many mutual friends and a common goal of getting to the party, there was no reason not to accept his offer. But when Margaret's recently acquired friend drove too quickly for the remote, dusty African village roads the car veered off, overturned and came to rest awkwardly upside down in a nearby field.

As night fell and the enormity of what had happened began to sink in, the two – strangers until a few hours earlier – faced very different outcomes. Margaret knew immediately something was terribly wrong. Her friend, meanwhile, scrambled unscathed from the remains of the battered vehicle. He wanted to walk back to the nearest village to call for help. Lying the wrong way up and in considerable pain, Margaret asked him not to, preferring he stayed close by. With no traffic or nearby houses to call upon the two remained alone together for hours until eventually, a passing lorry driver stopped and the alarm was raised.

Despite offers of help from local people who were now gathering at the scene, Margaret insisted on waiting for a doctor. 'I wouldn't let them move me,' she recalled. 'I knew something very serious was wrong.' When an ambulance and medical help did appear, the car first had to be turned the right way up before she could be set free. But the car, and Margaret, were precariously perched and, fearing further injury, a young policeman crawled into the vehicle and wedged his body against hers to keep it still for the difficult manoeuvre. It was, by all accounts, agonising.

From the crash scene Margaret was taken to a local hospital in nearby Lilongwe and some weeks later, to a bigger centre in Blantyre, now the country's second-biggest city. It was here that a surgeon was flown from South Africa to operate and Margaret was to learn for the first time that her spinal cord had been severed. She was paralysed from the point of the break, at T11 in the thoracic spine, down.

The Foreign Office sent word to Margaret's family back home but since travel was slow and prohibitively expensive, there was little they could do but wait. Visiting was out of the question. Two months later, in April 1959, she was declared fit enough to travel and a flight, paid for by the British Government, was arranged to take her home. 'I was told I was going to a very well-known hospital called Stoke Mandeville,' she recalls. 'It meant nothing to me.'

First, though, she had to endure a rather inelegant exit from the plane as the cockpit was dismantled to get the stretcher out. This was then placed on a truck and moved to a waiting ambulance. From the airport she was taken the relatively short distance to Stoke Mandeville Hospital in Aylesbury, Buckinghamshire, which had a specialist spinal unit.

And it was here that a very different journey, for Margaret Maughan and many others, would begin.

***

As an observer it's impossible to imagine what it must be like to walk out the door at the beginning of the day non-disabled and to find, by nightfall, you are disabled. And then to face the reality that life is irreversibly changed and there is nothing you, or medical intervention, can do. We get glimpses of it, mainly through the media, of someone in the public eye whose life changed because of a random, traumatic event, but that doesn't mean we understand its full impact.

For example, Christopher Reeve, best known for his role as the superhero Superman, broke his neck after being thrown from a horse in 1995 and became a quadriplegic. Or Formula One Team Manager Sir Frank Williams, who became a paraplegic after a crash in a rental car he was driving in France in 1986.

Who knows what coming to terms with the reality of a life changed forever is like, or the emotions inevitably brought up? But one thing is for sure: in those early hours and days, once survival has been established, the role of those most closely involved is vital.

Would hospital staff ever approach these cases with anything other than a positive outlook for the person in their care? The answer, of course, is no. And yet, inconceivable as it may seem to us today, as recently as the early 1940s patients with severe, traumatic spinal cord injuries were looked upon as poor, useless 'cripples' with no value to society in their new, injured form. It was believed nothing medically could be done to help them and so they were left to die. Average life expectancy after suffering a paralysing injury was only three years. The two big killers of the time were urinary tract infections, leading to kidney failure, and septicaemia. To make matters worse, patients were often left alone and, all too aware of their slim chances of survival, became deeply depressed.

But as the 1940s progressed and the Second World War dragged on, things were about to change. By 1943 the British Government were making plans for a push on the second front in the spring of the following year. The aim was for European forces to make one final effort to bring the war against Germany to its conclusion. The Government feared this would lead to an influx of men spinally injured from battle and in preparation, asked neurologist Ludwig Guttmann, a German émigré who fled to England with his wife and young family on the eve of the outbreak of war to be in charge of a specialist unit at Stoke Mandeville Hospital. Guttmann accepted on the condition he could put his theories, which he had been researching for many years, into practice without being challenged.

On 1 February 1944, the 26-bed unit opened to almost universal scepticism. It was called Ward X. Few could understand why Guttmann would, by choice, embark on such a career path. Ten years later, in 1954, the Superintendent Physiotherapist of the time, Dora Bell, reflected on what they all thought about it at the time: 'It is just 10 years that [sic] news filtered through that a ward was shortly to be opened for paraplegics, perhaps even two wards,' she wrote. 'What a soul-destroying thought. Should we hand in our resignations?'

One of Guttmann's first tasks was to challenge and alter the entrenched belief that a person with paraplegia – a loss of function of the lower limbs and trunk, usually caused as a result of injury to the spinal cord or because of a congenital condition, such as spina bifida – could only live a futile life.

When Guttmann arrived in Britain it was believed a paraplegic would never be capable of simple tasks such as getting dressed or putting on shoes, so what was the point of giving them any kind of physical rehabilitation in the first place? Guttmann fundamentally and consistently disagreed with this perception and, as a foreigner in a new job in a new land, had nothing to lose in trying out his own new methods.

These methods, including insisting patients be turned every two hours – to prevent pressure sores – and making them participate in a programme packed with various tasks and activities, were radical. And since it was still more than 30 years before the introduction of the Patient's Charter, they were also obligatory.

His motive was not to turn them into elite sports performers; after all, the Paralympic Games, as we now know them, were not even in existence. His motives were far more wide-reaching. He had a deep-rooted desire to rehabilitate each disabled person in his care, restore their independence and allow them an opportunity to learn a trade or skill, such as woodwork, clock repair or typing, so that when the time came for them to be discharged they would, once more, contribute to society in some purposeful way.

Guttmann also wanted to challenge the belief that the disabled were to be patronised and pitied rather than embraced as human beings with the same gifts, talents and worth as everyone else, non-disabled or not. And he knew that participating in sports activities was far more beneficial for the psyche than repetitive physiotherapy. 'The great advantage of sport over formal remedial exercise lies in its recreational value,' he said. 'By restoring that passion for playful activity – the desire to experience joy and pleasure in life – so deeply inherent in any human being.' And he knew then what we know today, which is that sport benefits all. 'The aims of sport for the disabled as well as the non-disabled are to develop mental activity, self-confidence, self-discipline, a competitive spirit and comradeship.'

One sporting activity patients had to participate in was archery. Not only did it help build strength and coordination, but it was also the perfect sport to help the paraplegic reintegrate into society, a key Guttmann aim. And, unlike other sports like swimming or wheelchair basketball, in archery the shooting 'line' is identical whether the archer stands or sits.

And so, for whatever reason, on 29 July 1948, exactly the same day more than 4,000 non-disabled athletes from 59 countries would take part in the Opening Ceremony of the XIV Olympic Games at Wembley, north-west London, Guttmann organised an archery competition between two teams of disabled ex-service personnel. On one side, a team from The Royal Star and Garter Home in Richmond, Surrey, on the other the Stoke Mandeville crew. In all, 14 ex-servicemen and two ex-servicewomen participated in the contest. The Royal Star and Garter won and was awarded the Archer Shield Trophy.

Whether organising the event was a brilliant piece of advance planning or just a coincidence that became more significant with the passage of time isn't clear, but this is the earliest example of sporting competition among people with a physical disability in Britain.

An early 1948 article entitled, 'Bus and Bowmen at Stoke Mandeville', published in *The Cord*, a journal for paraplegics, reports on the contest and pictures the eight-strong winning Royal Star and Garter team but makes no mention of the Olympic Games or the Opening Ceremony. 'Many old friends gathered for what was really the first paraplegic reunion in this country, and it was good to see how well many of those who had left hospital were getting on,' the article reported. 'The archery competition between teams from Stoke Mandeville and The [Royal] Star and Garter was held under the supervision of Mr Bilson, the Champion Archer of England, and was won by the visitors.'

It went on to say, 'The archers gave an impressive display and we hope they will soon have a chance of challenging American and Canadian paraplegics at this excellent sport.'

And so it was that two teams took part in one sport on one day in the summer of 1948, in what was called the Stoke Mandeville Games for the Paralysed; it was to change the course of disabled sports participation for ever.

Small as this inaugural event was, Guttmann knew it was a turning point. 'It was the first archery competition in the history of sport for the disabled. It was a demonstration to the public that competitive sport is not the prerogative of the non-disabled, but that the severely disabled, even those with paraplegia, can become sportsmen and women in their own right,' he said.

Initially, the event was a 'Sports Festival' but over time these summer sports gatherings became the Stoke Mandeville Games and they would happen every June. According to his daughter, Eva Loeffler, her father got rather carried away by the success of the second Games, in 1949, and uttered the now-famous words so often associated with his name: 'I prophesied that the time would come when this, the Mandeville Games, would achieve world fame as the disabled person's equivalent of the Olympics.'

According to Eva, since the assembled audience was made up of athletes, their helpers and family members no one present doubted her father's conviction. But some years later, writing in *The Cord* of 1964, Guttmann remembered the day he made that speech. 'Very few of those present shared my conviction, but nevertheless I never gave up hope that this dream would become reality,' he wrote confidently.

It was a confidence well placed for, sure enough, by 1952, within three years of making that speech, Guttmann was well on his way. The Medical Director of the Military Rehabilitation Centre in Doorn, Holland, asked if he could send a team to compete in the Games. Guttmann agreed and in 1952, his infant Stoke Mandeville Games had international representation, although the team from Holland came from a rehabilitation centre rather than, at that stage, being representative of the Dutch nation. In 1953, participants from North America took part as a team from Canada arrived and so the presence of international competitors grew.

Participants, and the sports they competed in, increased with every passing year, with the Stoke Mandeville team competing against teams from other spinal units around the UK. Once those Games were over, the best athletes would be picked to represent Great Britain at the Stoke Mandeville International Games, the forerunner to today's Paralympic Games. The International Games would be held each July.

It all began, though, in the grounds of Stoke Mandeville, when 14 men and two women shot arrows at a distant target. Out of doubt and despair, the tiny shoots of something positive and fulfilling began to emerge. Individuals, who only years earlier would have been written off and expected to die, were showing how powerfully transforming and empowering Guttmann's theories, once put into practice, were.

His vision had form.

***

When your world's been turned upside down by a life-altering accident you don't necessarily want to hear how lucky you are, but in Margaret Maughan's case there was a small element of luck on her side – Guttmann's rigorous approach to rehabilitation was in full swing when she arrived at Stoke Mandeville. And the first thing she noticed was how many others were in wheelchairs, a total novelty given her near isolation in Africa.

'My first experience, which was totally amazing, was lying in a bed in a ward of 20,' she says. 'It was so friendly. Everyone would get up and do all the daily things they had to and then young men would come in from other wards and everyone would go off to the pub in their wheelchairs. A lot of them were ex-service people, who had been injured in the war. In hospital the emphasis was on sport – everyone had to do it the whole day.'

Typically that would mean getting up and dressed for the day and then doing a skill-based class such as woodwork. This would be followed by swimming, physiotherapy and lunch. Afternoons would follow a similar pattern, with activities such as archery or table tennis and then further physio. 'By the time it got to 5pm, I was shattered,' she admits.

As Margaret got stronger, so she was encouraged to concentrate on what she could and would do in her future life rather than what she could not. There was no time for self-pity or despondency. 'You were encouraged not to feel sorry for yourself,' she says.

Despite the bonhomie of other patients and the packed daily schedule there were, inevitably, moments of physical pain and grief at a life irreversibly changed. In the early days of treatment patients had to spend six months lying in bed to allow broken bones to heal. To help this process and ensure the damaged spine remained straight during the initial healing period, hard sand bags would be placed end-to-end against the patient's spine.

Although necessary, it was also unbearably painful and uncomfortable, and it was during one of those periods, in great discomfort, Margaret began to cry. Just as she did a man she'd never met before appeared at her bedside: it was Guttmann. 'He told me I hadn't to be soft, but to be positive and not to give in to this,' she recalls. 'It was how my life went on from there – I am not a crier.'

On another occasion she made the mistake of telling Guttmann she was tired of lying in bed. His response was a 10-minute lecture, audible to everyone, on why she was on no account to be bored, but soon she had less time for this as her days became increasingly filled with activity. Then, one day, together with other patients, she was told to go to the back of the hospital, where something special was going on. She describes what she saw as, 'a strange collection of people from different countries in wheelchairs.'

It was the annual Stoke Mandeville International Games – and she had no idea she was about to be part of it.

According to Guttmann's PA Joan Scruton, it was in May 1959, not long after Margaret's repatriation, that the idea of holding these International Games outside the UK was first discussed. The Olympic Games were being held in Rome from late August in 1960 and Guttmann and his team talked with the Italian Istituto Nazionale Assicurazione contro gli Infortuni sul Lavoro, or INAIL, (a public body providing insurance for those who have accidents at work) and a spinal unit in Rome about holding the International Games in that city once the Olympic Games had ended.

The Italians were enthusiastic and over the months, plans took shape. After the Olympic Games ended, the wheelchair athletes would move in, with events being held on the nearby Acqua Acetosa sports ground, onto which athletes could easily push their own wheelchairs. In the early days it was only those with a spinal cord disability who competed. Other categories, such as athletes with a visual impairment, Amputees and Cerebral Palsy were not included for many years.

During 1959, word began to filter out about holding the Games in Italy and while much planning had to be undertaken, the news was met with excitement. 'The prospect of a meeting on the same spot as the Olympic Games as well as the wonderful journey to Rome brought imagination to a height,' wrote Andre Castello of the Swiss team.

Meanwhile, forced to take up archery as part of her rehabilitation, Margaret quickly discovered she was rather good and found herself winning the monthly competitions that took place. In December 1959, eight months after returning from Malawi, she was well enough to leave hospital and return to her parents' house in Preston. Nearby was a local club, Preston Archers, which Margaret joined and where she was immediately welcomed. 'I was the first disabled archer,' she recalls. 'I was a curiosity.' By June the following year, 1960, Maughan had been invited back to Stoke Mandeville to compete at archery in the National Games.

When Guttmann arranged the very first Archery competition in 1948 he was at pains to point out sport was for all, not only the elite and certainly not just for the non-disabled. For him participation was the most important factor and with this in mind, he ensured competitions were arranged into categories that ranged from 'beginner' to 'medium' and finally 'top' so that everyone could take part.

Participating in the middle group at the Stoke Mandeville Games, Margaret won, somewhat to her surprise. 'Nothing else was said and I went home,' she recalls. Some time later a letter arrived in the post inviting her to join a team going to Rome in the September. 'I didn't realise it was going to be such an important thing,' she says. 'To me it was just so exciting – I was going away again!'

The letter instructed her to turn up at Stoke Mandeville, which she did. There, according to her, a team of 70 assembled. All underwent a physical examination to make sure they had no pressure sores before being passed fit to travel. Each was issued with a woolly green tracksuit, a smart blazer for special occasions and a hat before being loaded onto a coach bound for Heathrow, known then as London Airport.

At the airport the coach drew up alongside a specially chartered plane that was waiting on the tarmac. The athletes were then individually lifted from their seats and carried to a catering truck, which was capable of transporting four wheelchairs at a time to the door of the plane. From there they were once again picked up and carried to their allotted seats. 'It took hours,' Margaret remembers, but despite the painstakingly slow process, the excitement was palpable. 'They made such a fuss of us,' she continued, 'and when we landed in Rome there were lots of photos.'

The XVII Olympic Games ended in Rome on 11 September 1960. A week later flags were still flying outside the Olympic Village as it prepared for the arrival of 400 disabled athletes and their assistants from nations representing all five continents: Argentina, Australia, Austria, Belgium, Canada, Finland, France, West Germany, Great Britain, Greece, Ireland, Israel, Italy, Lebanon, Malta, Norway, The Netherlands, South Rhodesia, Sweden, Switzerland, the USA and Yugoslavia.

Chapter One

The teams got together the money to pay for their travel to Rome in various ways – the Argentinians raised commercial funds and sold bonds during Wheelchair Basketball matches, while the Australians collected £10,000 through public subscription. And for some of the teams, just getting to Rome meant extremely lengthy journeys. The Argentinians spent 23 days at sea, while the Swiss travelled in groups by train and road, some of the latter detouring en route to take in a few of Italy's sights, such as Lake Maggiore and Venice, along the way.

An Irish team of five competitors – one woman and four men – arrived late after the captain of their Aer Lingus flight asked if they minded staying in Winterthur, near Zurich, for the night as he felt the weather to be too inclement to cross the Alps.

'Would we mind?' wrote Father Leo Close. 'We were delighted! A night in Switzerland at the expense of Aer Lingus – who would turn down an offer like that? To add to our enjoyment, Captain O'Callaghan of Aer Lingus, in typical Irish fashion, told us to be in no hurry in the morning, for we were so late now a few more hours would make no difference. We had a very pleasant night there and a lovely drive through the Swiss countryside to the Airport next morning.' Little did they realise just how lucky they were.

When the British team arrived at the Olympic Village they were in for a shock. The carefully planned, wheelchair-accessible rooms were no longer available and they instead found themselves accommodated in a rather less suitable block of flats, which were located on stilts. The rooms were only accessible by a dog-leg set of 16 steps or by a plywood ramp, which was far too steep for wheelchair athletes to push themselves up. Athletes could only get up if there was someone at the bottom who could carry them. 'I have never lost so much weight in so little time,' Jean Stone, who was one such carrier, recalls.

As it happened, Stone was only in Rome as a helper after the physiotherapist who was supposed to accompany the team fell downstairs the night before departure and broke her arm. She stepped in to help and so began an association with the Paralympic Games that has seen her attend every Games since, from 1960 to 2008. 'When I saw the accommodation I could not believe it,' she says.

Despite the setback the competitors took it all in good part. 'We were here to take part in the Stoke Mandeville Games on the same fields as had been used for the Olympiads, which we had all watched so closely on TV only recently,' wrote Malta's Victor P. Amato.

'The Olympic Village had sounded like fairy-land from afar, but it gave us a bit of a shock that first day when we found that we were going to live upstairs! How ever were we going to get up those ramps?' he continued. 'We had learned how to cope with difficulties, and we had come a long way, and nothing was going to be allowed to spoil our fun, so up those steps we got – wheelchairs and all – and in the end we learned to think nothing of it.'

Getting up and down the stairs was dealt with by some in a novel way. The Americans would use their chairs to 'bounce' down the stairs but they, like everyone else, still had to get back up them. So the Italian Organising Committee asked the army to step in and a timetable was arranged whereby soldiers were placed at the foot of each flight of stairs to carry competitors up and down, no matter how late at night. 'Wheelchair people are good at partying,' Margaret observes. 'They wouldn't be going to bed early.'

There were other challenges. Many doors were too narrow for wheelchair use, which meant the few bathrooms capable of accommodating wheels were occupied by many. 'It was all very communal,' continues Margaret. 'Someone would be in the bath and you would be on the loo at the same time or having a wash. We all got to know each other pretty well – you had to put up and make do.'

Another unplanned change was the announcement that the Acqua Acetosa sports ground would no longer be available. Instead, a new venue was found, which involved a 40-minute coach ride in each direction.

Glitches aside, after the Opening Ceremony on Sunday, 18 September, the Games began the following day with a programme of sports comprising: Archery, Wheelchair Basketball, Dartchery, Wheelchair Fencing, Athletics (Javelin, Precision Javelin, Shot Put, Indian Club Throwing), Snooker, Swimming, Table Tennis and Pentathlon. The Opening Ceremony took place on the warm-up track with tiered banking where spectators, including Jean Stone, stood. 'You did get the sense it was an occasion and something different,' she recalls, 'but it was very much the Stoke Mandeville Games being held in Rome rather than at Stoke, and Guttmann was in charge.' She also remembers many renditions of the Italian national anthem being played, repetitively, during the Opening Ceremony by the Italian Army band.

Once word had filtered out about the possibility of hosting the Games in Rome there had been some apprehension about moving to another location and whether it could emulate the facilities at Stoke Mandeville. The unsuitable accommodation and change of sports ground did little to alleviate any tension, but in the end no one need have worried. Apart from a deluge of rain on the first day, the weather was kind and a few language problems aside, the athletes forged friendships with each other and relished the opportunity to be alongside those who truly appreciated what it was like to be disabled.

As the new sports ground was so far from their accommodation all the competitors received a daily packed lunch. 'We thought they were very lovely,' says Margaret. 'They each had a little bottle of wine with it. In England you didn't do that kind of thing.'

In 1960, just to get into the team you had to participate in more than one sport. There were no sports specialists then. Margaret was doing Archery and Swimming. The first she loved, the second she didn't. 'I just wasn't good at it,' she reveals. 'I could only do backstroke.'

Archery, on the other hand, was an entirely different matter and the event took place on the opening day of the competition. Margaret was used to shooting three arrows at a time and then having these collected and returned for the next round, but in Rome six arrows were shot at once and quickly collected for competitors to shoot again. It was soon over and she was wheeled away to watch the other events without any idea of how she had done. When the day drew to a close, she returned to the coach that had brought her there. As usual, she was carried on board and her wheelchair folded up and put away with all the others. It was only then that an official announced she was needed and the whole process took place in reverse. 'To my total amazement I had won,' she recalls of her Paralympic success. 'I had got the gold medal. It was the first for Great Britain at that event and I was the first-ever gold medal winner, in any event for Britain.'

As she wheeled herself to the winner's rostrum she saw the British flag unfurled and heard the National Anthem played to all present. It was a magical moment. And while her medal was the first gold, it wasn't the only one: the team's final total was 20 gold, 15 silver and 20 bronze.

But it wasn't the only highlight for Margaret or the other 400 assembled athletes. Many would never forget being addressed by Pope John XXIII at Vatican City after the Games had ended:

Dear Children,

Recently, we welcomed at St Peter's Square athletes from all parts of the world, who came for the Olympic Games, and we felt a keen happiness in looking upon this ardent youth, who came to take part in these healthy and peaceful competitions of the stadium.

How much more moving for our hearts is the spectacle you offer to our eyes today! The weakening of your physical powers has not impaired your eagerness, and you have come to take part, in these recent days, with great enthusiasm in all kinds of games, the practice of which must have seemed to you for ever impossible.

You have given a great example, which we would like to emphasise, because it can give a lead to all: You have shown what an energetic soul can achieve, in spite of apparently insurmountable obstacles imposed by the body.

You are a living demonstration of the marvels of the virtue of energy.

Even this excitement was surpassed by some more personal attention, notably for Father Brendan O'Sullivan (a team escort) and Father Leo Close (competitor and unofficial team chaplain), who both had a private audience. 'When we are old and doddering, there will be one highlight of our trip to Rome that will remain always vivid in our memories – our audience with His Holiness Pope John XXIII,' Father Leo Close wrote. 'It was certainly an experience,' Stone recalls of the week-long event.

Buoyed by the moment, the British team left Rome on a high, which continued when they touched down in London, where Margaret Maughan was among the first to disembark to meet waiting photographers. 'It was so exciting,' she recalls. From London she completed the last part of her journey home to Preston, where she was warned the local press would be waiting for her.

Back then homecomings were a little less extravagant and more down-to-earth than recent times and it must have been something of an anticlimax after the excitement of Rome to board the train. Particularly as Margaret's seat, from London to Preston, was her own wheelchair loaded unceremoniously into the Guards Van. This is how Britain's first Paralympic athlete to become a gold medallist travelled home. Not that she was complaining: travelling for the first time since her accident, shooting against international competition and participating with hundreds of other athletes, let alone winning, marked the start of Great Britain's success at the Paralympic Games.

Apart from some organisational issues the Games were a resounding success, with many athletes reflecting on how inspired they felt at the possibilities the event had ignited in them and a resolve to return four years hence. There was also an overriding sense that the Games had shown, once more, how sport overcomes barriers. Many athletes left believing in a better future. Nizar Bissat, the first paraplegic to represent Lebanon, wrote, 'To the paraplegic hope is essential – it gives him courage, patience and the will to live.'

Holding the Games had, in his view, been a catalyst for far-reaching change. 'It has made many people talk about, and follow up news of the Games – especially those paraplegics all over the world who are very depressed and of low morale, and who have confined themselves to their own homes. By these means they will be encouraged to go outside their houses, forgetting their illness, and looking for a chance to join and cooperate in these Games. Thereby the aims of the Stoke Mandeville Games will be fulfilled.'

Ludwig Guttmann was also pleased with how the Games had unfolded: 'The first experiment to hold the Stoke Mandeville Games as an entity in another country, as an international sports festival comparable with the Olympic Games and other international sports events for the non-disabled, has been highly successful.'

And he was quick to establish his view on certain points that others had raised, during and after the Rome 1960 Games. In particular, he came under increasing pressure to open the Games to athletes other than those with spinal-cord injuries but he was adamant the Games would remain as they were and that new disability groups, and events, would not be admitted. Guttmann felt that if other groups joined the Games there would be fewer competitors with spinal-cord injuries; instead, he suggested they set up their own events.

'It is quite impossible to open the Stoke Mandeville Games to other forms of disability, such as amputees and the blind,' he wrote in *The Cord*. 'This really would be at the expense of the paraplegic sportsman, as it would immediately reduce the number of paralysed competitors who could be accommodated.' But by the time those IX Annual International Stoke Mandeville Games ended on 25 September 1960, change was in the pipeline. Today, just a half-century on, the Paralympic Games have become the world's second biggest multi-sports event after the Olympic Games. This has been, by any standards, a meteoric rise. Today we take for granted that every four years the Olympic Games will be held somewhere around the world and around a month later, the Paralympic Games will be held in the same city, using the same venues and accommodation.

Guttmann lived in an age with no wheelchair-accessible transport or public conveniences, no Disability Discrimination Act or political correctness and no equal opportunities. What is so remarkable is not just his commitment to changing society's view of the disabled but that he had – and held onto – his sporting dream, despite the prejudice.

Of his belief to create a Games that would, one day, be parallel to the Olympic Games there is no doubt, but in 1948, could anyone have envisioned that the Paralympic Games of the 21st century would have their own international stars, performing cyclically on a worldwide stage watched by a global audience eager for more? No, never.

Chapter Two

The Changing Games

**'Do not go where the path may lead,
go instead where there is no path
and leave a trail.'**

Ralph Waldo Emerson, essayist

Such is the pride that local people take in that fact Stoke Mandeville Hospital is the birthplace of the Paralympic Games that road signs have been erected along the county's borders informing motorists that they have entered 'Buckinghamshire – Birthplace of the Paralympics'. But from the moment the first Archery competition ended on that July day in 1948, the Games quickly evolved in terms of direction, understanding, athlete participation and sporting content.

At the first fully international Paralympic Games in Rome 1960, 400 athletes took part in nine sports. By the time London 2012 comes round, 4,200 athletes are expected to compete in 20 sports. This ten-fold increase in athletes in just over 50 years is immense by any measure. Part of the progression has come about because of the role of certain individuals as innovators, administrators and athletes – or all three.

Ludwig Guttmann is the obvious early innovator, but there have been others with visions of their own. As time has passed, the Games have become less about medical rehabilitation and increasingly about sporting excellence, until the Games of today which are, exclusively, about sport for elite athletes with a disability, held in the same facilities around the world as the Olympics.

But it's not just the gigantic, multinational Olympic and Paralympic Games of the modern era that take years of planning and coordination. Fifty years ago, when the Paralympic Movement was in its infancy and there were hundreds, not thousands of competitors, the need to organise and look ahead was no different. In fact, it was arguably more challenging, since long-distance air travel was neither as accessible nor as affordable as it is today, particularly for disabled travellers. And the next Paralympic Games would certainly test travel endurance limits to the max.

The 1964 Olympic Games were scheduled for Tokyo and Guttmann was keen to build on the success of the Rome 1960 Games and ensure the pattern of following the Olympic Games with the Paralympic Games continued. According to *The Cord* of 1964, even as events were unfolding on the sports ground at the Rome 1960 Games, discussions were taking place between Guttmann and Japanese delegates who had come to observe. Holding the Games in Asia would be another milestone, taking them outside Europe for the first time, and after the problems experienced in Italy, where the athletes had had to be carried up stairs to their accommodation, the International Stoke Mandeville Games Committee wanted to make sure that in Tokyo everything would be accessible.

In 1962, as dialogue between the two countries continued, two Japanese paraplegics made the long, arduous journey to Stoke Mandeville to compete in the 11th Annual International Games for the first time.

Their arrival took place the same year as Caz Walton (née Bryant), a 15-year-old with spina bifida, began a long and distinguished association with Paralympic sport. Selected to compete in eight Games, from Tokyo 1964 to Barcelona 1992, she clocked up 10 gold medals in Paralympic Athletics, Wheelchair Fencing, Table Tennis and Archery, was awarded an OBE for Services to Disability Sport and still works with ParalympicsGB today. After her competitive career ended, she continued to attend every Games in one capacity or another.

But it all started when Walton was a patient at Great Ormond Street Hospital in London, where she was told swimming would help her condition. After taking the advice offered by her physiotherapist at the time her parents took her to Stoke Mandeville, where she ended up competing in the National Games, which took place each June. Two years later, somewhat unexpectedly, Walton was asked to represent Britain at the Tokyo 1964 Games after a girl who was to have been in the team fell ill with three weeks to go. It was in Tokyo that she won her first two gold medals, although not in the pool but on the track. Today it might seem inconceivable to see an athlete first in the pool and then on the track in the same Games, but in the 1960s and 1970s doubling up, to compete in more than one sport was common practice. 'There was so little finance in those days we had to do more than one sport just to be considered for the team,' recalls Caz. 'The more the Games went on, the less there was a need to do multiple sports.'

Before departing for Tokyo she received a letter instructing her to meet at Stoke Mandeville, where specially acquired bottle-green uniforms were distributed. Tommy Taylor and Michael Beck, two quadriplegics, reflected on their newly acquired clothing with enthusiasm. 'Our uniform was a dark green blazer, white trousers and white shoes, not to forget the white hat! Fab gear!' they wrote in *The Cord* that year. White, though, is not a good colour for athletes in a wheelchair since any splash or dirt from wet and well-used roads or pathways would, inevitably, end up on their clothing, making it almost impossible to keep clean. And, unlike today, the kit wasn't theirs to keep: at the end of the Games it had to be returned, hung up and stored in Stoke Mandeville for use next time around.

Still, Taylor and Beck weren't complaining. Such was the severity of their disability they never imagined they would gain selection for Britain, let alone fly thousands of miles around the world, or be recipients of the £10 pocket money distributed to all team members by the Paraplegic Sports Endowment Fund, originally set up to ensure the Stoke Mandeville Games had a secure financial basis. They were thrilled that any of this was happening.

Getting to Tokyo required a major effort in itself as the chartered KLM flight had to refuel in Scotland before a journey that took around 22 hours, about 10 hours longer than it would today. And in some cases it required a huge effort just to get the athletes off the plane.

Jean Stone, who, as already mentioned, had attended the 1960 Games as a young helper for the British team and who later became involved with the International Paralympic Committee (IPC) as technical secretary of the Sports Council, remembers the moment two members of Japan's Self Defence Force arrived to lift one of the larger team members off the plane, only to realise they were not up to the challenge. 'They looked at the athlete, who must have been 18 or 19 stone, and then looked at each other and they could not keep their faces straight,' she recalls. 'They went away and came back with reinforcements.'

Once the team arrived, though, they found the Japanese friendly and polite towards their new guests, if bemused. In 1964, it wasn't common for wheelchair users to lead a normal life. 'In Japan if you went outside the Village they couldn't believe what they were seeing,' recalls Caz Walton. 'When you went abroad it was almost as if you had grown horns and arrived from Mars.'

Curiosity aside, the Japanese turned out to be admirable hosts. All the Olympic signage had gone, replaced by Paralympic signs showing a picture of wheelchair wheels. 'I have been to three Games in Asia and all three have been excellent,' says Caz. 'The hospitality has been second to none.'

The Games were opened in the presence of Crown Prince Akihito and Crown Princess Michiko (now the Emperor and Empress of Japan), who listened as the athlete oath, including an agreement for participants to conduct the Games in a spirit of 'friendship, unity and sportsmanship', was read out. For the athletes it was another memorable experience, reinforcing friendships, understanding and team spirit.

And at the end of it all, the white hats worn by the British team were in much demand. 'When the [Closing] Ceremony was over, the spectators wanted our hats as souvenirs, so we let them have them,' wrote Tommy Taylor and Michael Beck.

The 1964 Games boasted accommodation for the athletes in the same Village used by those competing in the Olympic Games a month earlier, on an old US Army base with single-level bungalows. It would be another 20 years before such parity was seen again.

Undoubtedly, for many of the 70 or so strong British Team of 1964, Tokyo was one big adventure with a few sporting events thrown in. And while the events the athletes competed in, such as Archery, Wheelchair Fencing, Swimming, Table Tennis and Athletics, were enjoyed, they were by no means the only memories the athletes came away with.

Take Daisy Flint, for example, a swimmer who later reflected on the real highlight of her Tokyo trip: a visit to the hairdressers. On the day of the Closing Ceremony, she and five teammates decided, as every self-respecting woman in their position would, that getting their hair done was a priority if they were to look their best later in the day. So off they went to a local salon where, having been treated like royalty, they were then told it was all on the house. But Daisy and the girls had spent a little too long under the dryers and when they emerged, realised there was no chance of getting back to the Village in time to be changed and ready for the Ceremony at 4.30pm.

Sensing the urgency, their interpreter got the girls back onto their special bus and then promptly disappeared out of the salon only to re-emerge some minutes later from the back of a police car. Then, with lights on and siren blaring, the car weaved a path through rush-hour traffic for the bus so the girls could get to the Ceremony on time. 'Sometimes I wonder if it all was not some marvellous dream,' a delighted Daisy wrote.

The party atmosphere did not end there. Back in the UK, then Prime Minister, Harold Wilson, invited them all to a reception at Number 10 Downing Street, creating yet another moment to savour for the returning athletes.

Chapter Two

Until the mid-1970s thousands of government-owned blue three-wheel trikes were supplied to the disabled so they could be independent and get around. These three-wheeled contraptions, with a tiller to steer and brake much like motorbike handles and an engine at the back, were widely regarded by the disabled and other road users as both lethal and unreliable. True to form, when the day came for the Number 10 reception, many guests decided to drive themselves to the heart of the British Government and park their trikes right outside. All went well until the time came for them to go home. 'One of the team couldn't get his trike started,' remembers Caz Walton, 'so he got one of the nearby Coppers to give him a push start.'

***

Within the medical confines of Stoke Mandeville Hospital Ludwig Guttmann was revered by his patients, who were eternally grateful for his interventions, which invariably saved them from near certain, premature death. Others marvelled at his desire to change society's view on the disabled, his boundless energy and a spirit undiminished by prejudice and negativity. 'Never' was not a word in the Guttmann vocabulary. Some, like Caz Walton, observed and enormously respected his presence even though she herself was not a Stoke Mandeville patient. 'He was a workaholic, and an autocrat,' she says. 'You always knew who was in charge. I admired him a lot: he inspired me, he was afraid of nothing. It did not matter what the problem was, he would tackle it. I never saw him despair of getting a result if that is what he thought was right. If it meant climbing Everest, he would do it.'

In the foreword to Susan Goodman's 1986 book, *Spirit of Stoke Mandeville,* the Prince of Wales himself wrote, 'No battle on behalf of his patients was too small to excite his complete interest and dedication. He was a man of genius and his personal warmth and humour were infectious.'

Although a short man with a very strong German accent he never lost, despite living more than 40 years in his adopted country, Guttmann was a big character. Whether his domineering, fearless approach came from his upbringing or that he survived unimaginable degradation and segregation as a Jew living in Nazi Germany in the years before the outbreak of the Second World War is unclear, but whatever the reasons he had, and never lost, a deep sense of humanity.

Born to an Orthodox Jewish family in Tost, Upper Silesia in Germany on 3 July 1899, the eldest of four and the only boy, Guttmann, although frequently described as 'autocratic' and 'stubborn', was a deeply compassionate man whose early life influenced his future career. When he was three, the family moved to the industrial town of Königshütte and it was here, in 1916, in the middle of the First World War, that his school class was asked to complete a population census. Guttmann was given the task of covering the coal-mining district and the poverty and deprivation discovered in the course of this exercise left a lasting impression on his conscience, as did his first encounter with paralysis, a year later, in 1917.

He volunteered as an orderly at the local Accident Hospital for Coalminers and he witnessed the arrival of a young coal miner, who had been paralysed from the waist down. As Guttmann began to show an interest in the man's condition, one doctor told him not to waste his time as the miner would be dead within six weeks. Five weeks later, after a series of urinary tract infections and pressure sores caused fatal sepsis, the miner died, an experience Guttmann never forgot. 'Although during future years of my career I saw many more such victims suffering the same fate, it was the picture of that young man which remained fixed in my memory,' he said.

After school he studied to be a doctor at the University of Breslau, combining his training with a passion for physical activity and sport, particularly fencing. By 1924, having passed his medical exams, he was looking for a job in general medicine when he was told by a friend there were no general vacancies and he should, instead, consider going to the 'floor below', where the department of Neurology and Neurosurgery had an opening. 'Somewhat dejectedly, I did. And perhaps more than any other, those words shaped my whole life and future career,' he later said. He took his friend's advice, was offered and accepted the job. It was this decision which ensured the rest of his career was devoted to neurology rather than in the service of paediatrics.

By 1933, conditions for Jews in Germany were becoming increasingly intolerable and Guttmann, who by now was working in a hospital in Breslau, lost his job. In the July he took up a position at the Jewish Hospital in Breslau, later becoming medical director. He was rising to the top of his field and hoped Hitler's grip would not last long, but by 1938, the net was tightening. First, he was ordered to discharge all non-Jews from the hospital and then, on 9 November 1938, he endured the infamous Kristallnacht (or 'Night of Broken Glass') when synagogues were ransacked and set on fire and thousands of Jews rounded up and sent to concentration camps.

On 9 November Guttmann instructed his staff to admit any males who presented themselves at the hospital, and more than 60 did. The following day, the Gestapo insisted on being told why there had been so many overnight admissions so Guttmann took them on a ward round, frequently inventing conditions as he moved from bed to bed so that the men could stay and be saved from the camps. In the end, only four were removed from his care.

By 1939, it was clear Guttmann would have to leave Germany. With an established international reputation, which had taken him to other countries to assist with complex cases, offers to work abroad were not in short supply. But he chose Britain. Guttmann finally arrived in England on 14 March 1939 with his wife Else and two young children, Dennis and Eva. The following day, Germany invaded Czechoslovakia and the turmoil of World War II was about to begin.

Initially Guttmann and his young family lived in Oxford, where he worked for many years on various research projects. Then, in 1943, he was asked if he wanted to run a new spinal unit, which was opening up in readiness for the anticipated war casualties. He accepted on condition that he could put his theories into practice unchallenged: his terms were met.

Despite official Government backing for his plans, Guttmann arrived at Stoke Mandeville to find himself swimming against a formidable tide of prejudice and defeatism. Even the nurses and physiotherapists viewed caring for paralysed patients as a lost cause. After all, even if the patients did survive, they would surely only be living out their days full of despair, or so it was believed. 'It is amazing to think that not many years ago, treatment of paraplegics was generally regarded as a waste of time,' The Prince of Wales wrote in his foreword to *Spirit of Stoke Mandeville.*

Guttmann's methods, and how life was for the disabled living in Britain in the 1940s, are documented elsewhere in medical and historical journals. Suffice to say, as his work took root and the cynicism around a long-term future for the disabled lessened, so the Games began to grow in size as the number of events contested and teams entered expanded. Guttmann always wanted Britain to field the biggest teams: whether it was his gratitude to the country that gave him and his family a new home or simply competitiveness, he was always keen for his adopted country to win most medals. 'His ambition was for us,' recalls Caz Walton, who experienced Guttmann first-hand. 'And he was very driven. He always thought of himself as British, or seemed to, and he would support us against Germany.'

At Stoke Mandeville Guttmann was rightly regarded as a saviour. Much to the surprise of his medical colleagues, he had taken on the least appealing area of medicine at the time – paraplegia – and embraced it with conviction, passion and an unshakeable belief in change.

But not everyone who made up the British Paralympic Team of the 1960s and 1970s came to it because they were patients at Stoke Mandeville. There were other spinal units around the country, such as Lodge Moor in Sheffield, Promenade Hospital, Southport, and Edenhall and Philipshill in Scotland. They had athletes and teams of their own, but not all of them shared a universal affection for Guttmann.

***

One man who wasn't a patient at Stoke Mandeville and felt the unyielding side of Guttmann was a young Philip Craven. Today, he is chairman of the International Paralympic Games (IPC) and a man who has had a huge impact on the direction of the modern Games.

Philip's story begins in Farnworth, near Bolton in Lancashire, where as a young boy growing up, he was talented enough to be asked by his school to represent them at swimming and tennis but sufficiently belligerent to decide early on he didn't like training and much preferred competing instead. It was a character trait that some years later, in entirely different circumstances, would stand him in very good stead.

Philip was passionate about football, spending hour after hour wearing out his shoes by kicking a ball around the yard. It was a commitment not matched by natural talent. 'I was useless,' he says.

In 1965, aged 15, football got a competitor for his time in fell walking, an activity he thoroughly enjoyed. So it was natural enough that rock climbing would inevitably follow and in September 1966, at the age of 16, he set off with some friends for Wilton Quarries, near Bolton, with its vast array of climbs for all abilities. The teenagers felt confident the Quarries would offer something suitable for them to practice on. Together, they chose a climb which didn't appear unduly difficult. It began well enough but before long became increasingly severe with a small stream running down from the top, which made conditions underfoot slippery and difficult for the boys to get a grip: Philip's friends were reluctant to carry on.

By way of encouragement he offered to lead and clear a path the others could then follow. Despite his lack of experience, he made the ascent with relative ease only to find himself face to face with a big rock. Checking it was stable enough to hold him, he pulled on the rock to make sure. The rock stayed firm, so Philip put his entire weight on it, expecting to be able to pull himself safely up. Instead the rock dislodged, taking him with it and back down the 10 metres he had just climbed. The ground beneath was uneven and as he landed on his hands and feet, he was thrown back, somersaulting onto a rock and breaking his back. The force of the fall was such that he blacked out and when he came round, he was so badly winded that he was sure he was about to die. It would be the last rock Philip Craven ever climbed. He was taken to hospital in Bolton and then, the following day, transferred to the North West Spinal Injuries Centre at Southport, where a long, four-month hospital stay began.

Some would regard being paralysed as a 16-year-old, on the verge of entering manhood and all that offers, as utterly devastating. For Hilda and Herbert Craven, Philip's parents, this was an unimaginable blow, particularly for Herbert. At a time when they thought their son was about to gain independence and go out into the world, suddenly they found themselves becoming increasingly protective and concerned for his future.

While Hilda set about reorganising the house to accommodate their son's new, less-mobile state, Herbert was in shock. 'My dad was struck asunder by it, even though he didn't show it,' Philip remembers. 'He was very affected by it.'

He himself, meanwhile, took a rather different approach. Initially, as he learnt how to manoeuvre his chair in and out of various everyday situations, he was reluctant to venture out and be seen outside his parents' house in the local community until he was more confident of his skills. Before long, he was getting out and about once more. 'I would get in my three-wheel trike and drive to Southport, which was 40 miles away, because nobody knew me there,' he says.

After about a year he had overcome his early inhibitions and was happy to be seen out and about in Farnworth. By now he had come to terms with having wheels instead of legs and decided to make the best of it. 'I found myself in a situation and I wanted to carry on living my life. At the age of 16, I probably didn't know what that life was going to be and maybe, that was a big benefit because I had more of a blank canvas. I wasn't married, didn't have a job and I was at a school I could go back to. I didn't think, "I am going to fight this", or have a reaction to the fact I was now living life in a wheelchair – I just knew I had to live with it,' he says.

The accident had another unexpected benefit. Since he had spent four months in hospital, he successfully argued he could never make up the time and should do two, rather than the then-standard three A-levels instead. 'Being Philip Craven, I did exactly what I wanted,' he says. By the time he did go back to school, he had an inkling sport was going to become increasingly central to his life. 'I could play sport and concentrate on something I already liked,' he said. Although he didn't realise it at the time, he had already glimpsed the sport he was to become so proficient at.

Just two days after his accident he had seen wheelchair basketball being played from his hospital window. He was captivated by the speed and excitement of it, although another year would pass before he tried the game for himself. But as soon as he did so, he was hooked – before long Philip was training and playing for Southport, the club attached to the Spinal Unit, where he went after his accident. In those days it was often spinal units that provided teams who played against other spinal units. In June 1967, less than a year after his accident, Philip made his first visit to Stoke Mandeville, where Southport was playing in the National Games. He also took part in Swimming and Slalom events, where participants navigate a series of obstacles in their chairs.

He was still only 17, young and inexperienced, and yet was surprised at the paternal way in which patients addressed Ludwig Guttmann. 'They were calling him Poppa Guttmann,' he says, adding, 'I was an independent individual, who did not like being told to do too much by anybody. To them, he was a Papa – someone who looked after you. At 17 or 18, I didn't want anyone looking after me.'

By 1968, Craven was playing wheelchair basketball but not yet well enough to be considered for the British team at the Paralympic Games, which, following the Games in Rome and Tokyo, were held in Tel Aviv, Israel that same year. This applied only to the Paralympic Games, however: the Olympic Games took place in Mexico City, but medical experts believed it would be too dangerous for paraplegics to live, and compete, at such high altitude, where oxygen was less readily available.

Instead, they arrived in Israel shortly after the end of the Arab/Israeli Six-Day War. According to competitor Caz Walton, the occasional dog-fight was still going on overhead. 'You could see the planes having a go at each other,' she recalls.

As each Paralympic Games took place, the organisers were learning a little more about what was needed and required at venues to ensure events for the athletes, and their carers, proceeded without incident. In Israel, this was still a work in progress.

The Opening Ceremony was held in Jerusalem and a long line of buses left Tel Aviv to get the athletes there on time. On arrival, some, understandably, needed to use the conveniences, which had been set up in special tents. Unfortunately, the Israelis misjudged the height of wheelchair athletes and completely forgot the helpers would not be in wheelchairs at all. As a result, instead of wheeling or walking into private tent facilities, many found their heads poking out of the top.

'They [the Israeli hosts] were a bit rough and ready,' recalls Walton. 'I did Table Tennis, Wheelchair Basketball and Pentathlon.'

Back home, in 1969, Philip Craven, now 19, began life as an undergraduate at Manchester University, where his interest in wheelchair basketball developed into something else. At the time Manchester University were national basketball champions and Philip would spend hours training alongside them, watching how they played the game, what worked and what didn't, and adapting skills from the stand-up game into shots and techniques of his own. Some of what he learned later stunned his wheelchair opponents. 'That is what transformed me into a great player,' he says.

And this was not just the arrogance of youth. Philip Craven became one of the finest wheelchair basketball players in the world, using weekdays to train and learn from the Manchester University team and weekends to play for Southport's wheelchair basketball team. Gerry Kinsella, an athlete born with polio and who first met Craven when he was 19, recalls a young man who was passionate about the sport and very good at it. 'Philip was an exceptional athlete,' Kinsella says. 'A lot of people did sport for therapeutic reasons, but he and I did it because we loved the game and wanted to be the best we could.'

With that in mind, Philip would spend hours learning how to master skills such as dribbling, passing, shooting and wheelchair control. Add to that determination, a willingness to learn and hours on court – week in, week out – and that's how he honed himself into a great player. 'I loved the sport and wanted to get as good as I could be,' he says. 'I trained three hours a day – I knew I was a good player.' Then, with court practice over, he would get staff at the McDougall Centre in Manchester to carry him up the stairs to finish his training with another hour in the pool. It was clear that he was putting in the effort needed to become a great sportsman.

Craven graduated from Manchester in 1972, the same year he made his first of five appearances for Britain at the Paralympic Games. The Games were held in Heidelberg, rather than Munich, where the Summer Olympic Games took place. In Heidelberg he competed in two sports, Swimming and Wheelchair Basketball.

By now truly world-class, Craven was approached at Heidelberg and asked if he would like to play for the French Wheelchair Basketball team, Club Olympique de Kerpape in Brittany. In November 1972, he accepted. Today we think nothing of sportsmen and women going abroad to further careers and salaries: Jonny Wilkinson plays for French rugby club Toulon, while 2009 World backstroke swimming champion Gemma Spofforth lives and trains in Florida and World Triathlon winner Tim Don spends much of his time preparing in Stellenbosch, South Africa. In Paralympic sport in 1972, it was almost certainly unheard of, though.

Kerpape had a rehabilitation centre where, for £90 a month, Craven would devise outdoor training circuits to help patients become competent in their chairs during the day. At night he would train with the Club. Apart from the experience, the move brought other unexpected, life-changing benefits, as it was here that he met his future wife Jocelyne, who was working as a physiotherapist at the same rehabilitation centre.

With plenty of international experience under his belt and two successful seasons in France completed, Craven returned to England in August 1974, having married Jocelyne in a fishing chapel in Brittany, just down the coast from the rehabilitation centre, and settled into a new job as a graduate management trainee with the National Coal Board, who were more than amenable in providing him with time off to compete. 'He was certainly one of the best players in the world,' says Gerry Kinsella. 'There were two or three others who would have been his equal, but none would have been better.' Great Britain, meanwhile, were already developing into a formidable international wheelchair basketball team. In 1971 and 1974, they were European Champions, while in 1973, they became inaugural winners of the Gold Cup, or World Championships.

In the summer of 1976, attention was turning towards the build-up to the Paralympic Games to be held in Toronto, Canada (rather than the Olympic city of Montreal). As a member of the successful World and European winning British team, Craven was looking forward to selection for Toronto, which was due to be announced at the end of the Stoke Mandeville Games in 1976, which both Philip and Jocelyne were attending. For him, selection seemed a formality.

At this point it must be remembered that Ludwig Guttmann and Philip Craven were both formidable, pioneering characters with passionate views, albeit from two different generations. So when one person such as Guttman, who started the Games, came up against someone like Craven, who was starting to formulate a view that the set-up needed to start changing, differences were inevitable.

This began one night while Philip and Jocelyne sat watching swimming events and the Team Manager came over to chat to them. Philip spoke frankly about his views, little knowing thus would have far-reaching consequences. The next morning he was summoned to appear before Guttmann, other Stoke Mandeville officials, the Team Manager and some of the coaches to explain his outburst. He repeated his belief that some coaches were incompetent and not up to the job. Guttmann, who was not used to having his authority challenged, was not amused. Craven recalls, 'He told me if I stepped out of line again between then and when the plane took off for Toronto, I would not be in the team whether I was one of the best players in the world or not. That was the end of it; there was no discussion.'

As it turned out, the British Wheelchair Basketball team, who were reigning European Champions, under-performed in Canada and returned home disappointed.

With the Games over, Philip was looking forward to his next involvement with the British team, which would be the European Championships, but months went by and he heard nothing. In those days teams did not train year round, as they do today, but even so he knew training days were due to be scheduled into everyone's diary. But still he heard nothing.

Finally, he approached the chairman of his club, Southport, and asked him to write to Guttmann to find out what was going on. According to Craven, Guttmann replied saying Philip Craven and Gerry Kinsella might be among the finest exponents of the game in the world, but since they were incapable of team play, they were banned for life – unless they apologised.

Kinsella never did play for Britain again and although wheelchair basketball was as important to him as it was to Philip, he was adamant he could not apologise: 'I am a stickler for principles. No one told me why I was banned. I refused to apologise.'

In the end the Craven's ban was of no consequence. According to him the performance of the British team declined, and both he and Kinsella were invited back into the fold. 'They realised they could not do without the two of us,' he says. 'I thought I would achieve more change from being within than being outside.' He could see that by getting involved as an administrator he could have huge influence and went on to be instrumental in changing the way wheelchair basketball athletes were classified so they were no longer dictated to by doctors but classified on a broader, more sport-specific basis.

By the late 1970s other athletes were starting to realise that they were only ever the recipients of services and not participants. Change was close at hand. According to Tony Sainsbury, who was Chef de Mission (or Team Manager) of the Great Britain Paralympic Team for five Games, from 1980 until 1996, athletes were already reacting to imposed rules. 'The athletes were always spoken to as patients,' he recalls. Then one night, after the 1979 Stoke Mandeville Games, according to Sainsbury, they decided it was time to party.

Plentiful supplies of alcohol were purchased and music set up in one of the tents used for Wheelchair Fencing during the Games. The beverages were ready and the music prepared when they realised they had nothing with which to illuminate proceedings so one car and one Toyota campervan were driven inside the open flat of the tent and left, engines running and lights glaring, to ensure the party went ahead. According to Sainsbury, when those who managed the Stoke Mandeville Games found out, technical officers were ordered to immediately shut down the party. The athletes protested and a disagreement ensued.

Parties or not, the Games, athletes and innovators were changing, and it wasn't just among athletes such as Craven and Kinsella that changes were afoot. There were also changes in the way the Paralympic Games were run and who could compete in them. From 1960 until 1972, the only athletes permitted to take part in the Paralympic Games had spinal cord injuries. A spinal cord injury can affect specific areas of the body; injuries sustained to the middle and lower areas of the spinal cord can cause paraplegia, where the lower limbs and all or part of the trunk are impaired. If the spinal cord is damaged further up the spine, in the neck, quadriplegia or tetraplegia may occur, where both upper and lower limbs are impaired. The way the athlete is classified refers to the area in the spine which is damaged. Conditions such as spina bifida and polio, where muscle function is impaired, also fall within this category.

In 1976, two more disability groups were added: athletes with a visual impairment, or blind athletes, and amputees. Athletes with a visual impairment covers all conditions which affect vision. There are different categories within this group, from those with a reduced visual field to total blindness. Amputees must be missing at least one joint or part of an extremity, such as an elbow, wrist, ankle or knee. Such losses can be congenital, from birth, or as a result of illness or accident. The classification of an amputee athlete depends on a number of factors, including whether it is an upper or lower limb impairment, whether a single limb is involved or multiple limbs and the location of the amputation – for example, above or below the knee. In 1976, these three disability groups made up the Paralympic Games.

***

As the 1970s progressed, Guttmann became increasingly elderly. He had, by now, received countless awards in recognition of his exceptional influence and work, including a Knighthood. In July 1979, a glittering 80th birthday party was held for him, where Prince Charles and several other celebrities were the guests of honour. It would be the last time they would all come together for him: in October of the same year he suffered a heart attack and died on 18 March 1980.

Even before his death the Paralympic Games were becoming less about rehabilitating patients after accidents and far more about individual performances in a variety of sports, a transformation reinforced by a number of polls carried out for the 1980 Games, which were held in Arnhem, Holland, rather than the Olympic city of Moscow. According to results published in a special commemorative book for the 1980 Games, a survey of 18 countries revealed little or no truth in the belief doctors were the driving force behind sport for athletes with a disability. According to the survey only eight per cent of athletes were urged by a doctor to take up sport, whereas 54 per cent were encouraged by relatives or friends.

Also in 1980, athletes with Cerebral Palsy (CP) were admitted to the Games. Cerebral Palsy is caused by of a lack of oxygen to the brain, which leads to damage affecting muscle tone, reflexes and posture or movement. The condition can occur before, or at birth, or following a stroke or head injury. Sufferers are classified differently depending on their level of impairment and which muscle groups are affected. The inclusion of CP athletes took the number of disability groups to four – spinal cord, athletes with a visual impairment, amputees and CP. And so the Games kept growing.

The 1984 Paralympic Games were supposed to be split between two American cities: Champaign, Illinois would host the wheelchair events and New York would host all the others. However, the Illinois part of the organisation suffered from funding problems and Stoke Mandeville stepped in at the last minute to take over. Although it was a huge task to take over from Illinois and agree to host the wheelchair events of the Games at Stoke Mandeville with only a few months notice, rather than the four years their predecessors had, as well as raise the funds required and organise accommodation for the athletes, everyone involved was determined that the Games should go on. And against the odds, they did. They were even opened, at very short notice, by Prince Charles.

This Games saw a fifth disability group added – 'Les Autres'. French for 'the others', Les Autres covers all athletes who do not fit into the other disability groups and include conditions such as arthrogryposis, multiple sclerosis and dwarfism. To top it all, the 1984 Games were the first where the IOC officially approved the use of the name Paralympic Games.

So the Games were expanding gradually but one edition changed the Paralympic experience forever – Seoul 1988. Without a doubt these more than any other Games that had gone before were a watershed moment in Paralympic history. Whether out of a sense of duty to the athletes or to their country, the Seoul Organising Committee embraced the challenge of hosting and welcoming Paralympic athletes.

'I will never, ever forget it,' says Tony Sainsbury, the British Chef de Mission in Korea. 'I remember being in the tunnel for the Opening Ceremony and walking out in front as the leader of our team into bright sunshine and seeing 80,000 screaming fans. I never imagined there would be more than 5,000 people watching, or to see such a magnificent stadium absolutely packed.' And he wasn't the only one who was overcome. 'As I looked around a lot of my team were crying,' he says. 'For the first time in history they had been recognised and identified in a sporting situation.'

But it wasn't just the athletes who were affected: up in the stands those who had followed the Paralympic Movement from the outset were struggling with their own emotions. 'The Olympic Stadium was full,' recalls Jean Stone. 'I had a tear in my eye seeing the teams come out and hearing the noise – I had been to some Games when it had been silent.'

As the Games unfolded, the Koreans delivered sell-out crowds at the various venues, day after day. How they achieved this – by enlisting church communities and schoolchildren and assigning different countries for each group to support – was less important than the impact on all who experienced it. 'I don't think the Koreans knew who they were cheering for, but they cheered. The place was heaving and it was what they, the athletes, had always hoped for,' Sainsbury recalls.

The Seoul Games were significant for another reason, as never again would the Paralympic Games be held in a different city to the Olympic Games. Twenty-eight years after the first Games for athletes with a disability were held outside the UK in Rome in 1960, and nearly 30 years after 'that' Guttmann speech, his desire for disabled athletes to be alongside, or parallel, to the Olympic Games had finally been achieved.

Between 1988 and 1992 standards went up again in terms of organisation and athlete performance. The professionalism seen in Barcelona in 1992 had raised the organisational side of the Games to a new benchmark level, so Atlanta 1996 had a tough act to follow. But the Games took a temporary dip in terms of the quality of the facilities athletes had now come to expect and this inevitably impacted on the competitors. This illustrates how fastidious the organisers have to be to keep on top of the number of potential problems associated with the presence of so many people in one place: getting things wrong inevitably attracts criticism.

For Tanni Grey-Thompson, who retired in 2007 after a glittering career spanning five Games (1988–2004) and 11 Paralympic gold medals, Atlanta 1996 was the third of the five Games she had attended as an athlete. She was not impressed with the set-up. 'I was sharing a room with another wheelchair user and it was tiny. We had to move the wardrobe out into the communal area and place kit on the bottom of the bed – there was no room for two wheelchairs,' she says. 'They used part of the Olympic Village but once the Olympics were over, they started to take it down.'

According to Jean Stone, now at her 10th Games, Atlanta 1996 felt underwhelming. 'It was a blip,' she says. There was little link between the Organising Committees of the two Games, which had consequences for the smooth-running of the event. 'The accommodation was the same, but there was no handover,' she continues. 'All the keys for the rooms were in a big biscuit box and they had to spend hours sorting through the keys to find which ones fitted which rooms.

'When the officials arrived there were beds, but no linen or pillows,' she recalls. 'The catering facilities were placed at the top of a hill (which made wheelchair access hard). The drivers were volunteers and struggled with the ever-changing traffic system.' Spectator numbers were also lower than in previous Games, which made it difficult to generate atmosphere in the venues. 'In Barcelona, people had queued to get in. I could not believe it,' Stone says. 'In Atlanta, I don't think the stadium was even full for the Opening Ceremony.'

Although Atlanta 1996 attracted less credit than Barcelona, at least the Paralympic Games ensured the continuity of the movement and the principle of holding the Games in the same city as the Olympic Games. The Atlanta Games also saw the sixth and, so far, final disability group admitted for the first time: Athletes with an Intellectual Disability (ID). Intellectual Disability refers to athletes with a cognitive impairment that affects an individual's ability to deal with life's everyday challenges. However, the inclusion of ID athletes turned out to be short-lived.

Whether the young Spanish journalist Carlos Ribagorda had any idea of the impact his actions or story would eventually have, when in the months before the Sydney 2000 Paralympic Games he joined and trained with the Spanish Basketball team with Intellectual Disabilities, even though he himself had no disability, seems unlikely but the scandal he subsequently wrote about had repercussions for all athletes with an intellectual disability that today has been rectified.

Ribagorda went to Sydney and helped the Spanish Basketball team reach the final, where they crushed the Russians by 87 points to 63 to take gold. Spain rejoiced – but not for long. In the weeks that followed Ribagorda broke the story that 10 of the 12 team members, including himself, were, in fact, not mentally impaired and did not meet the necessary qualification criteria to be there, which included having an IQ of less than 75. Ribagorda also claimed the practice of selecting athletes with no actual disability took place in other Spanish Paralympic sports, including Athletics, Table Tennis and Swimming.

Although the allegations were initially denied, an investigation corroborated Ribagorda's findings. Two key Spanish officials were expelled from the IPC, who made it clear this type of deceit would not be tolerated. The Spanish Basketball team gave back their gold medals but the damage, for ID athletes, was done.

It was clear that new processes needed to be implemented to verify an athlete's disability within the sport they wished to compete in and until those processes could be tried and tested, the decisive step was made in 2001 to remove the ID category from the Paralympic programme. The six disability groups were five once more.

But by November 2009, it was clear that the new measures for assessing ID athletes were now robust enough for the IPC to announce that ID competitors would be returning to the Paralympic Games in London 2012 in three sports – Athletics, Swimming and Table Tennis – ending their 12-year absence. And so, competitors from six disability groups are expected to participate in the 20 existing sports making up the Paralympic programme. There are no debut sports for 2012, but Rio 2016 can look forward to two new ones – Para Canoe and Para-Triathlon, taking the total to 22. How the Games have moved on.

***

There was of course mutual respect between Ludwig Guttmann and Philip Craven, both of whom, for different reasons, in different times, have left their mark on the Paralympic Movement. They may have clashed but both shared a desire to improve the lives of the disabled community. Guttmann approached it from a medical viewpoint, Craven from his perspective as an athlete first and administrator second.

It was fortunate that Guttmann's lifetime ban on Philip Craven was short-lived. Had it not been, the Paralympic Movement would have lost one of its brightest lights.

Like Guttmann, Craven believes everyone should enjoy the benefits sport offers regardless of race, colour, creed or ability. 'The greatest benefit of sport without a doubt is sport for all,' he says. 'Guttmann thought if you concentrated on elite sport it would stop mass participation – I do not believe that is the case.'

But Craven has enshrined something else in the IPC traditions and values – the desire of athletes at the Paralympic Games to be recognised as elite performers with a disability, and nothing more. He grasped this better than anyone else because as a young man he was driven to excel in every area of wheelchair basketball; he set the bar of achievement and excellence for himself high and expected others on his team to do the same. 'He pushed himself,' says Kinsella. 'If he was in a team and they weren't taking it seriously, he would sometimes voice his opinion. But that inner strength and determination is Philip.'

Both Guttmann and Craven shared an understanding of the benefits sport has on society, and the ability it has to change the lives of the individuals affected and all around them. Craven knows its effect because it is the life he has lived since the age of 16. He was an athlete who dazzled opponents, amassing a staggering 192 caps for Britain. He once scored 26 points in a single match against the United States, ensuring they were well and truly beaten in a game they invented. 'They talk about being in the zone,' he says. 'You are only ever in the zone once or twice in your career. It is when you are on automatic pilot and can do whatever you have trained for and it happens perfectly. It was 1986 when I played that game for Britain and scored 26 points – I never slept that night.'

Craven was a tenacious administrator, overseeing the successful implementation of a new Wheelchair Basketball classification system, whereby athletes were classified on a broader, more sport-specific basis, which propelled the sport into a different, internationally respected footing. He went on to become President of the International Wheelchair Basketball Federation from 1988–2002.

In 2001 Philip Craven stood for President of the IPC, the international governing body of the Paralympic Movement, which was founded in Dusseldorf, Germany in 1989. Successfully appointed and then re-elected in 2005 and 2009, he is now in his third term of office, which ends in 2013. He has steered the IPC into the 21st century through controversy and change, and towards a future where the Paralympic Games are fully understood as being an elite sporting event. If he succeeds in the latter and oversees a sea change in awareness before his term of office ends in 2013, this may well be his finest achievement because to do so still requires an extraordinary transition in the way the watching public see, understand and appreciate Paralympic sport.

Craven's example and his own journey, from cocky youngster to one of the most influential people in international multi-sport, makes his message both compelling and engaging, as Baroness Sue Campbell, Chair of UK Sport since 2003 and herself a highly experienced figure in sport at all levels, has seen first-hand. 'When you meet Philip, you meet this forthright, articulate, formidable personality,' she says. 'I have watched him transfix audiences. He has a bluntness, a directness, which made people think very hard. I don't think he is afraid to stand up for what he believes in. He has strong values and he carried those into the IPC role.'

She added, 'The thing that shines out of Philip is his understanding of the power of sport in terms of how he found, or re-found, a sense of direction and purpose through sport. He really believes in sport as a way of shaping lives. You sense he sees this as a fundamental part of enabling people with disabilities to take their rightful place in community and society. That comes through like a light when he is talking.'

Campbell believes it's his straight talking, 'this-is-who-I-am' approach which has such power: 'As he speaks, and communicates, that piece of the human spirit shines in him in a way which is quite distinctive. It does not matter that he is bull-doggy and belligerent, and all those other things. Something shines in him, and still does, and it is a defiance which says damn it, I will and damn it, I am going to. He has done it and you have to admire and respect that completely.'

Whether he would accept the observations of others is unknown. There is no doubt, though, in his lifetime Philip Craven has helped bring about important, enduring and inspiring change in the Paralympic Movement.

When Guttmann died in 1980, Craven chose not to attend his funeral. They may not have shared a friendship, but they did share a passion to empower and engender respect for those with a disability. Were Guttmann alive today, he may have recognised that Craven ultimately held the same values as he did.

Chapter Three

Standing Out From the Crowd

'We are all meant to shine, as children do. And as we let our own light shine, we unconsciously give other people permission to do the same.'

Marianne Williamson, author

There are some athletes who might have gone on to achieve sporting greatness no matter what their circumstance: there is something about the qualities they exude that sets them apart. It is their single-minded focus, attention to detail or willingness to push personal and physical boundaries – or probably a combination of all three – that makes them special. But there are a select few whose influence is felt for reasons other than simple athletic success, whose stories stay in the heart and mind long after the victory ceremonies have finished. Their qualities manifest themselves in different ways. Some may show an unexpected warmth and (sometimes dark) humour that puts others at their ease. Others may pioneer new ways in which to perform a sport, and then set new benchmarks in it, as if to prove their point. Whatever their qualities, all these athletes are linked by a common thread: in one way or another, they all stand out.

***

When Sulwen and Peter Grey discovered their daughter Carys had spina bifida they couldn't possibly have imagined that one day she would do more than any other person of her generation to move public awareness and understanding of sport for disabled people to a new level. Nor would they have dreamed that the name Tanni Grey, later Grey-Thompson when she married husband Ian in May 1999, would become inexorably linked with elite sport, or that her 'there's nothing walking would give me I don't already have' approach to disability was, in part at least, down to their huge influence.

In the early 1970s, Sulwen and Peter approached Carys' upbringing, growing up near Cardiff, in exactly the same way they had her older sister, Sian. But first they had to get used to calling her Tanni. When Sian first saw her newborn baby sister she called her 'tiny' but it sounded like Tanni and the name stuck. In fact, if either parent attempted to call Tanni, 'Carys', Sian would scream the place down.

Spina bifida means 'split spine', and although Tanni had a relatively mild form, her condition was complicated and exacerbated by a curvature of the spine. The fact she survived childhood at all was a not inconsiderable achievement since most children born with the condition before the 1970s died within the first year of life. Tanni had ankle-to-thigh callipers to help her get around, but nonetheless her walking deteriorated over time and by the age of seven she increasingly needed to use a wheelchair.

Even before the change to using a wheelchair came about, her father, Peter, an architect, was aware that the environment they then lived in was both inaccessible and inhospitable to wheelchair users. There were many everyday obstacles to navigate, as well as those further afield. They couldn't go to the cinema as a family because wheelchairs were regarded as a fire risk and a day out they could all enjoy would be one where Tanni would not be in a panic trying to find a toilet. In the early 1970s, wheelchair-accessible conveniences did not exist.

But if it bothered Peter Grey, he never showed it. Instead he instilled in his daughter a lasting, far-sighted belief that the world would have to change to accommodate her and not the other way around. There was, he repeatedly told her, absolutely nothing wrong with growing up in a wheelchair. 'In those days disabled people were locked away, ghettoised and hidden from view,' recalls Tanni, 'but Mum and Dad were just these two incredibly positive people. It is just the way they were.' Peter also never made it out to be a big deal. 'I don't remember Mum and Dad ever talking about me being in a chair,' says Tanni.

Nevertheless it can't have been easy to hear, at the end of a working day, that other mothers had deliberately pushed their children out of the way of Tanni in the local supermarket for fear they might catch something. Or that a child at the Girls' Brigade called their daughter, 'Limpy Legs'. Mind you, Tanni's reaction to this particular childhood experience was pretty emphatic: she simply refused to go back.

Throughout it all, Sulwen and Peter remained steadfast. Such behaviour was not their problem but rather the ill-informed attitude of others. 'Mum and Dad never saw the chair. I didn't grow up thinking I was disabled because they never let anyone patronise or discriminate against me,' says Tanni.

Initially, her parents involved her in sport for exactly the same reasons all children engage in it: exercise is good for you, it builds confidence, coordination and teamwork, and in Tanni's case, it would improve her strength, which as a very young child was lacking. So, Tanni swam and went horse riding, played basketball and participated in archery. It probably helped that Dewi Thomas, her headmaster at Birchgrove Primary School, insisted, in an age long before inclusivity became law, Tanni be involved in all PE activities. He also refused to tell anyone in authority that she was in a wheelchair, knowing if he did, she would be removed and sent to a special school instead. 'He was very protective,' says Tanni.

Being born into a family of sports fans would undoubtedly have had an influence on Tanni's outlook. 'Dad played cricket and golf quite a lot and was a huge sports fan. As a family we watched a lot of rugby and football, and whatever other sports were on TV at the time,' she remembers. Watching was one thing, but even as a youngster Tanni preferred participating to pontificating on the performances of others.

As Tanni's primary school education came to an end there was still the issue of where to go next. The local secondary school, where all her friends were going, refused to accept her on the grounds it wasn't wheelchair accessible. In reality, though, this was her first real experience of discrimination.

In the early 1980s disabled children didn't usually go into mainstream education: they went to special schools, and that's what the Local Education Authority wanted for Tanni. But it wasn't what Peter Grey wanted for his daughter. Both he and Sulwen knew what the special system offered and it was not appropriate. After all, it was Tanni's body that was impaired, not her brain and a proper education wasn't a luxury, it was her right.

Peter studied the Warnock Report on special education – the White Paper for the 1981 Education Act – and his perseverance paid off. Buried somewhere in it, he found a line which said every child had the right to be taught in an environment best suited to their educational needs. It was this argument he successfully used to secure a place for Tanni at St Cyres Comprehensive in Penarth. It was an extra nine miles in each direction than the journey to the local secondary school would have been, but it was still a milestone in Tanni's life. And there was another gift that emerged from the process.

Being called 'Limpy Legs' was an unpleasant, passing experience but not the end of the world but going to the wrong secondary school would have been catastrophic. Tanni's parents had demonstrated the importance of picking the right battles.

As it happened, St Cyres was right next door to a special school and when their summer sports day took place, Tanni joined in. She already swam at St Cyres but here at the special school were other children in wheelchairs and with that came the chance to compete against them. One of Tanni's first races was the 60m, which she won. It may have been an inauspicious start to her wheelchair athletics career but much to Tanni's surprise, she enjoyed both the experience and the competition.

So it was with more than a little interest that the sports-mad Grey family settled down for the Opening Ceremony of the Los Angeles 1984 Olympic Games and watched American Rafer Johnson, the 1960 Olympic Decathlon champion, ascend a steep, moving staircase to the top of the stadium, from where he lit the Olympic Flame. As the festival of sport unfolded, they watched American Ed Moses win the 400m

Hurdles and Britain's Sebastian Coe become the first man ever to win successive 1500m Olympic titles.

More than 20 years later, when Coe made his impassioned final speech to the International Olympic Committee in Singapore in 2005 as head of the London 2012 bid delegation, he told the audience about the moment that shaped his life. He was 12 in the summer of 1968 when, along with his classmates, he was taken into a large school hall to watch images from the Mexico City 1968 Games beamed back onto an old black-and-white TV. Two athletes, husband and wife John and Sheila Sherwood, from Coe's hometown of Sheffield, were competing. John won bronze in the 400m Hurdles and Sheila silver in the Long Jump. 'By the time I was back in my classroom, I knew what I wanted to do and what I wanted to be,' Coe told delegates.

And yet his own performance in Los Angeles, along with others, impacted on a young Tanni Grey. By the time the 1984 Games were over, she too knew what she wanted to do. 'I wanted to be an athlete,' she says, although back then it was as likely to be wheelchair basketball or archery as it was athletics.

Tanni had sporting talent, of that there was no doubt. And had she been born without an impairment she would, in all probability, still have been a world-class sportswoman but most likely, in cycling rather than athletics. Back then, though, it would be a few more years yet before she settled on her chosen sport. And not until she was 22 did she decide that being the very best in the world at wheelchair racing was her destiny.

If Tanni was to take on the world's best she needed to be in an environment geared to winning, which is why, in the late 1980s, she picked Loughborough University as the next stop on her sporting and educational journey. Almost as soon as she arrived, she encountered various hurdles. The athletics track was hard to access and while there was a ramp, it could only be used if Tanni phoned ahead and requested a special gate be opened for her. And then there were the attitudes of the other athletes themselves.

Turning up for one circuit-training session Tanni was greeted by a young track runner, who informed her the session was for athletes. 'I know, I do wheelchair racing,' she responded. But the runner was unconvinced and told her they would be climbing up ropes as part of the session. Tanni simply got out of her chair and using the strength in her upper body, shimmied up to the top of the rope without so much as taking breath. Point proven, Tanni got on with her training, but it was a lonely, often unfriendly environment and since most of the conditioning work revolved around building leg strength, it wasn't relevant. 'I did some training with the athletics club, but it wasn't that helpful,' she says. In the end, thanks to the suggestion of a university friend, she ended up joining the mountaineering club, which was far more conducive to the type of strength and conditioning training she needed to do.

By 1988 Tanni was competing in the national championships using her first-ever racing wheelchair, provided by a charity, and making something of a name for herself in the wheelchair-racing world. By the time she arrived home from Loughborough at the end of her first year, she found a letter inviting her to represent Great Britain at the Seoul Paralympic Games.

But it was still only 1988 and the Paralympic Movement was in its infancy. Seoul 1988 would be only the seventh games since Rome in 1960 and only the fourth to admit amputees and athletes with a visual impairment. Tanni was entered in the Athletics 100m, 200m, 400m and Slalom, as well as Wheelchair Basketball, and returned with a bronze for the 400m. As yet, few outside the Paralympic movement had heard of Tanni Grey, but the medal from Seoul was proof indeed that the talent first shown in Wales a decade earlier had already translated onto a world stage. But this was just the beginning and there was so much more to come.

By the time Tanni got home from Seoul all she could think of was how to be a better athlete in the remaining three and a half years before selection for the Barcelona 1992 Paralympic Games. She didn't want to be patted on the head or thought of as brave and wonderful. Quite the contrary – all she wanted to do was train harder, smarter and more effectively than her rivals.

She imagined she'd race for a year or two and then be forced to get a well-paid job to provide her with enough income to pay for all the travel costs needed to train and race at the top level. As it happened, she won enough money in that first year not to need a full-time job and her clean sweep at the Barcelona 1992 Games, where she won the 100m, 200m, 400m and 800m on the track, ensured this arrangement would continue.

Although success in Spain marked her arrival on the international sporting stage, there was no danger of it going to her head. At major championships Tanni's father, Peter, and sister, Sian, were frequent track-side spectators but not her mother, Sulwen, who found the races unbearably tense to watch so would often stay at home, where she could better keep her nerves under control. Tanni was competing in the heats of the 400m, which she won. The shock was not the ease with which she crossed the line, but the time on the scoreboard: 59.20. It was a new world record and the first time a woman had broken the one-minute barrier for one lap of the track. Bursting with excitement, she rang home to tell her mother. 'I have just broken the 400m world record,' she blurted out. But Sulwen was unimpressed: Tanni had been shown spitting a mouthful of water onto the track, as many athletes routinely do. As far as she was concerned, world record or not, this was unacceptable behaviour and she made it clear. 'There is no need to spit on the track, you know,' she told her.

The four gold medals Tanni won in Barcelona were just the beginning as she went on to win 11 in total (a number since matched by swimmer Dave Roberts, who intends to beat that tally at London 2012). Her achievements have earned her the affection and respect of the sporting community and British public alike but her post-athletics influence does not end there as she is now Baroness Grey-Thompson, an independent Crossbench Peer, who sits in the House of Lords.

Many people would assume that growing up in a wheelchair sets a young person apart from their contemporaries through disadvantage. Tanni has shown how she has been set apart for other, more positive and enlightening reasons.

***

At Athens 2004, as Tanni Grey-Thompson was winning her 11th and final gold medal of her career, another member of the British team – Lee Pearson – was making headlines of his own.

Chapter Three

Pearson is a man who loves to talk. Whether it's about the time he offered to give HM the Queen a horse-riding lesson when they were introduced, or the day, as a young boy, when Margaret Thatcher carried him into Number 10 Downing Street, or what it means to be in total harmony with the horses he has ridden to World and Paralympic glory, Lee is rarely lost for words. He is an effervescent, engaging character, with a gift for putting others at ease.

So the gesture he made at Athens 2004 to a fellow competitor should not have come as too much of a surprise to those who know him. Lee won the Mixed Dressage Championship gold, but after being presented with his medal, he dismounted and made his way, on the crutches he relies on to get around, to the French teenage rider, Valérie Salles, whose horse, Arestote, had collapsed and died of a heart attack as they entered the arena to compete. He gave Valérie his winner's flowers. It was one of the most poignant and generous moments of the Athens Games, felt by everybody who saw it.

Although the sport's governing body, the FEI, awarded Lee a Fair Play Certificate and he was also shortlisted for the prestigious Laureus Sports Awards, his actions had been entirely spontaneous. It was simply a genuine gesture from one rider to another who was grieving a sudden, devastating loss.

It was all a long way from where life started out for Lee. Born in 1974, he had his left leg wrapped around his right knee, his right leg wrapped around his left knee and the umbilical cord around his neck. He also had a birthmark across half his face and part of his head. The hospital staff decided the best place to put such an usual-looking baby was in the broom cupboard.

Whether it was because they didn't want to upset other parents or because they themselves were not sure how to react, history does not relate, but Lee Pearson began life in a cot, covered with a blanket, and placed between a hospital collection of mops, brooms and buckets.

To begin with his mother Lynda was kept sedated, probably for fear of how she would react, but the day after the birth she threatened to scream the place down unless someone took her to see her son. Lynda, a psychiatric nurse, knew whatever she saw before her that day, she needed to respond positively or risk the baby being taken away. So, surrounded by an entourage of doctors, nurses and psychologists, she was wheeled to where the mops and buckets lived and introduced to her son. While inwardly her heart skipped several beats, she did exactly what any other mother of a newborn would: she picked up her son and gave him the first of many hugs.

Lee was born with arthrogryposis multiplex congenital, a rare, unusual condition, which affects more than 260 babies every year in the UK. Arthyrogryposis means 'curved joint' and results in the joints becoming fixed, or stuck, in a curved position in the womb, which prevents proper growth and range of movement. The earlier this starts in the growing foetus, the more severe the impairment will become. 'While normal muscles grow like an elastic band, my muscles grew like string,' says Pearson.

There are around 200 different conditions that fall under the umbrella term, although 'Arthyrogryposis', which affects all four limbs and which Lee has, is the most common. Lynda and Lee's father Dave, a lorry driver, could do nothing about the cause of their son's birth defects but they had plenty of say about, and influence over, what happened next.

'Mum and Dad decided they would give me everything I needed to put me on par with my two older brothers, Damien and Darren – no more, no less,' says Lee. 'My mum will tell you now she has three sons and she loves them all the same. She was no less proud of me when I could not do things and she is no more proud of me now.'

Like her other sons, Lynda Pearson wanted Lee to lead as full a life as his brothers. Before he could even be considered for sporting activity the doctors wanted to try and flatten out his limbs, which meant 15 operations before the age of five and being placed on a crucifix, his hips and legs encased in plaster, to assist the process. This was agony for him. 'I used to scream and cry, and ask Mum why she was letting the doctors do this to me,' he recalls.

He was nominated for one of the Woman's Own Children of Courage awards and in 1980, aged six, invited to the annual ceremony. There he was introduced to John Thaw and his actress wife, Sheila Hancock, and to comedians Morecambe and Wise, before winning over the Prime Minister at the time, Margaret Thatcher. Britain's first female PM insisted she carried him up the steps of Number 10 Downing Street, even though he was quite heavy. Any offers of help from Dave Pearson were rejected.

Despite being in and out of hospital for years, Lynda and Dave resisted the temptation to pamper Lee. His parents wanted as normal a life as possible for him, and they wanted it to be fun. They got a bike with no pedals and pushed him down the hill and then put him on a motorbike, making sure they were on hand to catch him as his feet could not touch the ground. When the older two boys wanted to go waterskiing, Dave got a piece of plywood, modified it to fit Lee's size and he cut down a pair of wellies to provide greater stability. He was nine when Lynda, herself terrified of horses, introduced him to riding at a local centre where, according to his mother, Lee took a shine to a jet-black pony called Duke. Lee went to a normal secondary school, where he had little difficulty making friends, almost certainly because he knew how to use his humour to make other people feel comfortable if they were unsettled by his disability. He quickly learnt that if people were ignorant about his condition he needed to educate them, whereas if they were arrogant he needed to give as good as he got – which he usually did. And probably because of his own outgoing personality and general acceptance among friends, prejudice was rare.

Then, one December, Lee, Damien and Darren had a Christmas none would easily forget. While the two older boys discovered they now owned a new tractor and monkey bike, Lee was grappling to understand his collection of presents, which included a set of horse brushes, a bridle and a saddle, all of which were readily available at weekly riding lessons. When he asked his mother why she had made the purchases, she invited him to go outside. 'It was the most exciting and surreal day of my life,' says Lee, as he opened the door to find a horse box waiting for him. As the back came down, out came Duke, the pony he'd been having lessons on.

Lee uses splints, which run the length of both legs, as well as crutches, to get around; he has no strength in his legs or arms. To control a horse he relies on the exceptional balance learned as a child in those early days, which began with Duke. Given that Dressage, both for athletes with a physical disability and the non-disabled, requires the tiniest movements, executed with an expert technique and a unique understanding between horse and rider, did Lee find Duke responding instantly to his commands that Christmas morning? And was it the start of an effortless journey from pet pony to Paralympic podium? Not quite. 'I was absolutely rubbish, I would fall off every day! I was in so much of a panic. And Duke put me off riding for at least five years. By the time I was 10, I never wanted to see him again,' says Pearson. By the following Christmas, Duke had been sold. Lee still loved horses but his interest was on the wane.

Eventually, though, he did get back in the saddle, found a new teacher (Elsie Wilkinson) who drew out the horsemanship in him and, in time, never looked back. Of course, there were setbacks along the way: he fell off, frequently, but was more terrified of Elsie's reaction than the pain of the fall, so usually got swiftly back in the saddle. And he did a job he hated for six years, in order to support himself as he certainly wasn't good enough at that point to consider a professional career riding horses. Today, though, Lee Pearson is unquestionably the world's most successful Paralympic Equestrian rider.

Dressage is the only Equestrian event on the Paralympic programme and consists of a series of tests. The number of tests a rider completes depends on whether they are doing just an individual event, or the team event as well. If doing all three, as in Lee's case, first up is the Team Test, then the Championships Test, both of which involve riders completing a series of movements within a set amount of time. Each movement is awarded a score from 0–10 by a panel of judges, producing a percentage score for each Test. The length of the test varies according to a rider's disability and the category they compete in but will be between three-and-a-half and six minutes in Paralympic competitions.

The third, and final challenge is the Freestyle Test, where each rider completes a given number of movements, incorporated in any order they wish, to music of their choice. This test tends to be shorter than both Team and Championship Tests. Again, a panel of judges scores each movement to arrive at an overall percentage score.

Lee's first Paralympic Games appearance was at Sydney 2000, where he won three gold medals. At Athens 2004, it was three more and at Beijing 2008, his collection grew by another three, which meant he set an Equestrian Paralympic record for being unbeaten at three Paralympic Games. Symbolically, he's going for three more at London 2012, or, if successful, "12 in 12".

Lee only learnt of the Paralympic Games by watching it at home on his television. Perhaps the images helped provide the possibility of an escape route from a life he felt trapped in at the time. But perhaps, with his personality, he might have found his way into something he enjoyed more anyway. Either way, Lee Pearson is an athlete who is hard to forget.

***

Just as Lee Pearson has devoted the last decade to running his yard and preparing for successive Games, Richard Whitehead is a man with a serious passion. His one is an unquenchable desire to run. Not just any old distance, though. He wants to run that most gruelling of all races and one already hard enough for anyone with fully functioning legs – the Marathon. But Richard, a congenital double amputee, has no legs below the patella, or knee.

Although he's now found his true event, he has experimented with a number of different sports – including Ice Sledge Hockey – to find the one he feels most comfortable competing in. When he was four, he learnt to swim but he didn't like it and used to scream. He stuck at it, however, and whether because of the upper body strength he developed, or his natural aptitude, he was good. At around the same time his parents – Geraldine, a housewife, and John, a mechanic – realised sport afforded their son a unique opportunity to integrate with other children and to overcome boundaries which might, later on, have become a problem. 'They were very forward thinking,' says Richard. 'They could see sport would help me make friends and jump over barriers at an early age.'

Geraldine and John heard about a local gym club, Dako, in Nottingham, which not only put on acrobatic displays but also served the local community by providing young boys with an opportunity to learn a positive skill rather than the alternative of hanging around on street corners. Certain this could help, they enrolled Richard at the age of eight. He'd already tried most sports on offer but taking up gymnastics proved to be an insightful decision. For much of the next four years he would spend hours perfecting skills like balance, coordination, discipline and agility.

As gymnastics relies largely on upper body conditioning, he found he wasn't at as much of a disadvantage as he might have been in other sports. 'Gymnastics is made up of events like the rings, parallel bars and the pommel horse, and you don't need legs to do that,' he says.

But as is the case for any athlete, as Richard grew up there was the inevitable competition for his time. As his swimming improved, he had to choose to concentrate on one of the two sports much of his early life revolved around. In gymnastics he was good enough to be in the regional squad, while in swimming the possibility of international competition and travel beckoned. He chose the pool. And although gymnastics would no longer be a part of his life, he learned invaluable, transferable skills that have never left him.

A year later, at the World Youth Games in Miami (an event for disabled young athletes), he won five gold medals and one bronze. Not bad for a boy with no legs but it was not enough to make the endless hours of training and competition and the many sacrifices worthwhile. 'People would say to me you are an amazing athlete, you just haven't found your sport,' says Richard, and although he continued to swim throughout the junior ranks and into senior competition, in the end, as with gymnastics, he gave it up.

So often in sport it is the extraordinary feats of those competing half a continent away that inspire people to change something in their own lives, to be more committed or focused, or to concentrate on setting and achieving a specific goal. For Paralympic athletes the initial process is no different, and for Richard Whitehead it was watching a film about Terry Fox that planted a kernel of an idea.

Fox was a Canadian runner who, having been diagnosed with cancer, lost his right leg in the late 1970s. He then attempted to run across Canada to raise money and awareness for cancer research. Although he failed to finish the cross-country run and subsequently died from his illness, his efforts captivated Canadians and sparked a worldwide movement, which generated millions in cash for charity and touched countless people across the world.

Chapter Three

By the mid-1990s, Whitehead's dream was to be able to run on prosthetic legs. The technology existed but the price tag was prohibitive. And then, thanks to the help of a company that designs and makes prosthetics, a pair of running 'feet' were donated. Those 'feet' enabled him to run and so eventually he took to the streets of New York City for his first marathon in 2004. His time was 5 hours and 19 minutes. After this, his finishing times started to fall dramatically. In 2009, he became the first leg amputee to break the three-hour barrier, finishing in 2:56:45. He has since lowered that world record to 2:42:52.

Having proved he could become the fastest man in the world, Richard wanted to test this at the ultimate sporting event for disabled athletes, the Paralympic Games. As a double-leg amputee he is classified as a T42 runner, but there is no Marathon at London 2012 for this category because there are not enough elite-level athletes to make a competition viable or credible. So Richard asked the International Paralympic Committee (IPC) if he could race against athletes in the T46 category, which is for arm amputees, at the IPC Athletics World Championships in Christchurch, New Zealand of 2011. This category does have the Marathon event: at London 2012. However, the IPC are committed to ensuring there is a level playing field with athletes competing fairly against other athletes with the same impairment so his request was denied. But true to form, Whitehead's talent is such that as well as being a long-distance runner, he can also sprint. At the World Championships in New Zealand, in the absence of a Marathon race, he took to the track and won the 200m. His dream of running at the Paralympic Games is very much alive and he will be looking to gain selection to race on the track, particularly over 200m. So whether

Whitehead runs long and slow, or short and fast, he has become one of the most recognisable talents in Paralympic sport.

***

Martine Wright would not have chosen to have been catapulted into the spotlight as the 2012 Games approach or once they begin, but all that changed on the morning of 7 July 2005 when she boarded a Circle Line tube train and ended up sitting three feet away from the suicide bomber, Shehzad Tanweer.

She wouldn't have been on that tube at all had she stuck to her usual routine but the night before she'd been out with friends celebrating the news that London had won the right to host the 2012 Games. She'd been late home and on the morning of 7 July turned her alarm clock off to allow for an extra 10 minutes of snooze time. By the time she did get to the platform, late for work, she jumped on the first train and immersed herself in the day's paper, which was full of stories about London's jubilant win.

Somewhere though, between Liverpool Street and Aldgate stations there was, without warning, a white flash and Martine found herself in the black, acrid remains of a bombed tube carriage. It was the first of the four explosions to go off. Such was the extent of her injuries she was the last to be evacuated and might never have pulled through but for the quick thinking of an off-duty policewoman who made Martine tie something around her leg to staunch the flow of blood. It was this rough-and-ready tourniquet which undoubtedly saved her life. Even so, she entered a coma for over a week and almost died. When she did come round, she realised that under the hospital bed sheet, both her legs had been amputated.

Over time, as Martine recovered, she tried a number of sports including sitting volleyball which, unlike other sports, involves players sitting on the floor and not being in their chairs. Something about the liberation of it all appealed and now, unbelievably, she's in line for selection for London 2012.

In July 2012, as Britain prepares for the eyes of the world to be focused on the London Olympic and Paralympic Games it will also be seven years since 52 people lost their lives in the 7/7 bombings, seven of which were on the Aldgate train. Martine Wright could so easily have been one of them. There is an irony about the fact that celebrating winning the event inadvertently caused her to become part of it. Her presence at the Games will stand out as a symbol of courage and hope, proving how sport empowers and heals even after the darkest moments.

Chapter Four

In Search of Gold

**'Success is a journey, not a destination.
The doing is often more important
than the outcome.'**

Arthur Ashe, tennis player

It is vital to ongoing success that people with a disability who are good at sport find their way into the Paralympic system and have their potential nurtured. In many cases, whether an athlete is born with a disability or becomes disabled later in life, the process begins in the same time-honoured way – with sporting activity being prescribed for rehabilitation purposes. It could be a physiotherapist who recommends swimming to keep compromised joints supple, or riding to improve strength, balance, coordination and confidence. This is where many stories start.

But it's a long, painstaking journey from the first few strokes in a pool or sessions on horseback to becoming a proficient competitor. As an athlete's career progresses, disabled or not, they face questions over their commitment, attitude, professionalism and ability to deliver world-class performances under immense pressure. But athletes with a disability have the additional responsibility of managing their impairment on a daily basis. How much management is needed differs depending on the complexity and severity of the disability.

For some athletes the sheer physical and mental effort of surviving childbirth and the first few weeks of life is triumph enough no matter what they go on to do in the remainder of their lives. When Sophie Christiansen came into the world, rather earlier than planned on the afternoon of 14 November 1987, she was born premature, at just 32 weeks. In the month that followed she endured a heart attack, lung collapse and septicaemia. The doctors didn't hold out much hope. They drew the screens round, told Caroline and Karl, Sophie's parents, she would not last the day and asked if they would like her christened. They discussed funeral arrangements and how the process would unfold.

It was during one such discussion that Sophie must have decided they were missing the point. 'She opened her eyes and looked at me,' says Karl. 'It was as if she were saying, "what are you fussed about?"' And while there have been plenty of twists and turns since that November day, Sophie's earliest communication turned out to be an accurate reflection of how she, and her parents, approach life.

Sophie was later diagnosed with Cerebral Palsy (CP), the result of damage to the brain that usually occurs before, during or soon after birth. One of the tests she had to complete was to place different shaped bricks into the right shaped holes. To those watching it was obvious, much to Sophie's frustration, that she could see which hole was right but her fingers could not react successfully to complete the task. This was one of the early tell-tale signs of Cerebral Palsy.

There are various causes for CP, which include infection in early pregnancy or a difficult or premature birth. Around one in every 400 children in the UK are born with Cerebral Palsy and approximately

1,800 babies a year are diagnosed with the condition. There is, to date, no known cure and while not progressive it is neurological, which means it affects movement, coordination and speech. There are a number of forms, from the mildest, spastic hemiplegia, which results in muscle stiffness on one side of the body and potential curvature of the spine, to spastic quadriplegia, the most severe form, where the child is unable to walk or support their neck and may have moderate or extensive learning difficulties. Sophie has a mild form of the most severe category. All four of her limbs are affected, hence the term quadriplegia.

By the time Caroline and Karl had been given the official diagnosis Sophie was approaching two years old and the Christiansens were getting on with life in the way their infant daughter needed. In reality, they didn't know any different; few of their immediate friends had had a family at this point so they had nothing to compare Sophie's progress with. 'I am the oldest of three daughters,' said Caroline. 'None of my friends [or family] had babies at the time – I just don't think we knew what normal parenthood was.' As far as they could tell, developmentally at least, Sophie was only a couple of months behind other babies her age and that could easily have been put down to her premature birth.

As both Caroline and Karl were teachers, they felt well equipped to deal with any learning difficulties Sophie might have. They certainly didn't see the situation as either a barrier or insurmountable problem for the future.

As often happens, for disabled or non-disabled children it is the suggestion, or intervention, of an individual or organisation that sets a child on a certain path. And that was what happened to Sophie. While undoubtedly helped by her parents' approach, it was by no means the only factor in her later sporting success. For a start, the area of Berkshire she grew up in had a progressive approach to disability.

When Sophie was two and a half, Caroline fell pregnant with her second child, Alex. The local authority also recommended that from September 1990, when Sophie was just under three years old, that she attend the nursery unit at Whitelocke School (now called All Saints), an ordinary school in Wokingham. 'I think they felt it would be good for me to have a reasonably normal end-of-pregnancy and for Sophie to have some stimulation,' says Caroline.

Caroline expected Sophie to scream and cry and have to be prized from her arm when the first day of term came, but Sophie, who in those days had a little walker with wheels at the front to help her get around, went down the path, turned and shouted chirpily, 'Bye, Mum!' and headed off.

There was another significant benefit to attending Whitelocke – it had a special unit for those children who needed it. It meant Sophie had the best of both worlds and was gradually integrated into every aspect of school life. And then at the age of six the physiotherapists introduced Sophie to a new activity that would alter the course of the rest of her life: they took her riding.

Whether it was the area of the country Sophie was born in, a change in attitude towards disability or simply a growing awareness of the positive benefits sport offers all children, disabled or not, by the 1990s, the end result was greater opportunity in all. And Sophie Christiansen was by no means the only beneficiary.

Sophie was six when she learned to ride; Ellie Simmonds was younger still, just four, when she joined Boldmere Swimming Club in Sutton Coldfield, near her home in Walsall, where she gradually progressed from the steps to the pool. But it certainly wasn't love at first splash, as she hated getting her face wet and liked backstroke even less.

Nonetheless Ellie was a good swimmer and as she got older, she wanted to swim in galas like her other, taller friends. Born with achondroplasia – or dwarfism – Ellie never saw herself as any different from anyone else. She certainly didn't regard herself as small, which meant that if her friends were taking part in galas she wanted to participate, too.

One gala followed another and Ellie was getting well and truly beaten. It wasn't until she raced against other disabled children that her parents realised how good she was. By the time Ellie was nine, like so many other distinguished Olympic and Paralympic athletes who have been inspired by watching elite athletes perform via their television screens, she knew what she wanted to do.

Watching the Athens 2004 Paralympic Games at home in Walsall, Ellie saw Welsh swimmer Nyree Lewis win the 100m Backstroke S6 event, in a new Paralympic Games record, and then win a second gold in the 4 x 50m Medley Relay, as well as two silver medals and one bronze. Ellie Simmonds thought she could do that, too.

Three years later, aged 12, her talent established, Ellie was in the Great Britain development squad. A year after that she went from total obscurity to becoming the very public face of British Paralympic sport in the space of a few weeks.

Ellie was supposed to go to Beijing 2008 for the experience, so that when the time came for her to compete in London in 2012, the occasion would not overwhelm her. Clearly no one told 13-year-old Ellie the plan or, if they did, she ignored them.

First, she won the 100m Freestyle S6, then followed it up with gold in the longer 400m Freestyle S6 in a new world record time. It made her Britain's youngest-ever winner of an individual Paralympic Games gold medal. 'I have dreamed of being a Paralympic medallist but didn't think it would happen yet,' she says. The second gold had a twist to the tale as in winning the 400m Freestyle she beat Nyree Lewis, the swimmer who had inspired her four years earlier.

Simmonds' spectacular performances in the water, along with the tears of happiness that flowed from the victory podium, became some of the most enduring and endearing images of the Beijing 2008 Paralympic Games. But it didn't stop there. The teenager picked up the BBC's Young Sports Personality of the Year award at the December television showpiece, earned some extra local popularity by switching on Walsall's Christmas lights and then, to cap it all, was awarded an MBE for services to disabled sport in the 2009 New Year's Honours List. It made her the youngest recipient since Order of the Empire awards were introduced in 1917. And then she went back to what she was doing before – studying at school; not that being in a classroom or, in fact, any other post-Beijing experience, would ever be quite the same again.

Such recognition would have been unthinkable in the early days of disability sport, when the main function was to encourage the disabled, particularly those with severed spinal cords, to reintegrate themselves into society and contribute in a meaningful way. But Ellie Simmonds proved the Paralympic Games had become an event with the capacity to catapult successful participants onto a national and international stage. And, in Britain at least, there are established structures in place to identify and nurture potential from a very young age.

The British Paralympic Association (BPA), the organisation that leads Paralympic sport in the UK and is also responsible for ParalympicsGB at the Games, operates a number of schemes to uncover future athletes including Talent Identification Days, where athletes with a disability can try a number of sports under one roof. If successful, they are invited back for further trials and possible inclusion in the Great Britain squad. Talent Identification opportunities now exist in all Paralympic sports in some capacity.

Some sports, including Cycling and Rowing, offer fully integrated training programmes, where athletes with a disability regularly train alongside their non-disabled counterparts, often in shared venues. So, for example, the GB Para-Cycling Team trains with the non-disabled team at Manchester Velodrome, just as adaptive rowers use the same Caversham facility as Olympic squad rowers. Other sports, notably Equestrian, have their own tried-and-tested ways of spotting riders with the capability to go the Paralympic distance. It is, perhaps, no coincidence then that Cycling, Equestrian and Rowing were Britain's most successful sports at the Beijing Games 2008, with the British topping the medal table in each sport.

***

Sophie Christiansen started riding at six at a specialist riding centre close to her school because the physiotherapists knew the positive benefits it has for those with disabilities. There is something in the way a horse walks which increases sensation in the human body and as a result, improves mobility, balance and coordination. It is known to help with all physical disabilities.

No one could have imagined how much Sophie would love the experience or how quickly she would take to riding horses. Before long she'd persuaded Caroline to take her for a second weekly lesson, which at less than five pounds a time proved very affordable. 'It was all outdoors then,' says Sophie, 'so it was a big commitment for my mum. She would take me every Friday, whether it rained or snowed. That's dedication!'

By the age of 13, the riding centre Sophie was having lessons at felt her potential exceeded their resources and suggested she move to more advanced stables. As Caroline and Karl set about researching possible options they discovered they were within relatively easy reach of the South Buckinghamshire Riding for the Disabled Association (SBRDA). It was a huge stroke of luck. SBRDA is, unquestionably, one of the best riding associations for the disabled in Britain, if not the world.

Founded in the 1960s, the charity RDA has consistently and successfully delivered therapeutic enjoyment to thousands of disabled people of all ages for over four decades. It currently has more than 18,000 volunteers throughout the UK and, annually, encourages and introduces around 28,000 disabled people to the joys of riding. The RDA system is also one of the main ways in which talented British riders come to the attention of the sport's governing body. Other routes include year-round competitions and talent spotting days.

Associations like the RDA were inspired by Danish rider Lis Hartel, who was paralysed below the knees by polio when she was 23. Hartel was already a successful dressage rider when the disease struck, after which she was advised to give up riding. But she was determined to ride again and at the highest level. Competing for Denmark, she won two Olympic silver medals in Dressage, first at the Helsinki Games in 1952 and then four years later at the Stockholm Games in 1956, an extraordinary achievement for a rider with a disability. At Helsinki 1952 she was lifted from her horse by the legendary Swedish rider, Henri Saint Cyr, who, having won the competition, gallantly carried her to the podium for the victory ceremony. It was memorable not just because of his gesture but because Lis Hartel became the first woman in history to win an Olympic medal in Equestrian and share the Olympic podium with men.

Hartel had proved conclusively the therapeutic benefits of riding and her example inspired the creation of riding centres for the disabled in other parts of the world, including the UK. Over the years, the SBRDA has risen to the forefront of Paralympic training, with superb facilities, including an indoor school, and now has a long and hugely successful association with the Paralympic Games through the many riders it has helped reach elite level.

The Christiansens may not have realised it at the time but joining the SBRDA would be a turning point in Sophie's transition from keen rider to full international sportswoman. Apart from the facilities, enthusiasm, commitment and skill, the SBRDA was peerless in progressing riders with the most severe disabilities and they had the track record to prove it.

At the Paralympic Games, each competitor's mobility, strength and coordination are assessed in order to establish their classification. Riders with similar functional ability are grouped into competition Grades. These range from Grade 1 for the most severely impaired, to Grade IV for the least impaired; Grade 1 is further divided into Grades 1a and 1b. The competition within each Grade can therefore be judged on the skill of the individual competitor on their horse, regardless of the competitor's disability.

Christiansen's classification is at the very highest level of impairment, 1a, while Lee Pearson, Britain's best known and most successful Paralympic rider with nine gold medals, is 1b. 'In the world of Para-Equestrian we are rather good at helping those with the highest disability levels,' Caroline Christiansen says. 'Her [Sophie's] disability was her ability.'

Within a year of beginning to ride at SBRDA, Sophie Christiansen was put on the World Class Start Development programme run by UK Sport, which provides funding to help cover training and living costs. She was on disability's fast track for elite sport.

In 2003, then 15, Sophie was asked to represent Great Britain in Madrid, Spain in a low-key Dressage international. Britain took two teams to the event, a First and Second team, with Sophie selected for the First team. They won, and Sophie had her first international medal. She also finished runner-up in the Individual competition.

It was all valuable experience and the only time in her career she used what was called a 'borrowed horse'. The term 'borrowed' meant riders drew lots for their horse from a common pool; the same process also existed at the Paralympic Games and the host nation was tasked with providing horses for all competitors. There would be a pool of horses and the Chef d'Equipe (Equestrian Team Manager) would draw lots for their team members. It was a similar system to the one used for Modern Pentathlon in the Olympic Games, where riders drew lots for the horse they then rode in competition. As the selection process is random, no one knows which mount they will get and this creates a level playing field for all. 'Sophie drew Dote, an Andalucian stallion,' recalls Caroline Christiansen. 'I was terrified, but he was absolutely lovely to her.'

By now the Athens 2004 Games was on the horizon but first Christiansen had to find a horse of her own to compete on as the system for accessing horses was changing. From Athens 2004 onwards, Paralympic Equestrian would become an event where competitors took part on horses they supplied themselves rather than ones 'borrowed' at random from the Organising Committee of the day.

This change might have been a challenge, not just for Britain, but for teams around the world without the necessary resources to be able to raise the tens of thousands of pounds needed to buy an elite horse. Luckily, over the years, the British team has been aided by generous individuals who have provided a string of horses for riders to use. It was as a result of one of these benefactors that Sophie found a horse for Athens 2004. Britain's riding elite is a small, well-connected group and it became apparent that Nicola Tustain (another highly successful British Paralympic rider and double gold medallist from Sydney 2000) had a possible solution – Hot Stuff, who was both good enough and available. So, Sophie headed to Wales for a week to give the horse a try and a fledgling partnership was formed.

'Because I can't afford to own my own horse I do rely on other people's goodwill,' she says. 'I form a professional relationship with my horse, rather than the sort of relationship you have with a pet because I know it's not mine and I have to give it back,' adding, 'One of my skills as a rider is that I can ride any horse and get the most out of him for what I need.'

Next stop was the Athens 2004 Paralympic Games, if only for the experience. Sophie Christiansen was still only 16.

Athens 2004 proved life changing, but it wasn't just Sophie who was affected: all four Christiansens were. At three years Sophie's junior, Alex Christiansen, who was 13 when he travelled to Greece, had grown up knowing his sister was disabled but also not knowing any different. Helping her eat or walk was part of normal life and whether because of his gentleness or her initial dependency, they formed a close bond. 'When she is away at university now, I really miss her,' he says, 'but don't tell her that!' As he grew older, and more protective, he would react at society's prejudice towards a sibling who walked, and talked, differently. 'I was annoyed by people who stopped and stared when I was younger,' he says, 'but now I understand some people are just not exposed to it.'

And he never felt embarrassed or awkward, in fact the opposite. 'I was proud of the fact she was disabled because it gave me another knowledge base I knew about that others didn't,' he says.

In a family where one child is disabled it is easy for the others to feel overlooked, as Alex did when he first started at the same secondary school, Charters in Sunningdale, Sophie attended but not because she was disabled. 'It was because she was an international athlete!' he says. 'I did feel as if I was always her brother until I developed my own interests and people got to know me.' In fact he went on to become one of the head boys at Charters, which has since become a specialist Sports and Science College.

Inevitably in the early days whatever the family did revolved around the additional care Sophie needed. Every day either Caroline or Karl would stretch her hamstrings and Achilles tendons in order to make walking easier. Without their daily attention the muscles would have shortened and she would have ended up walking on her toes, a classic symptom of Cerebral Palsy. And whether it was watching this ritual, or the years of compassion, patience and wisdom gained from growing up with a disabled sibling, when Alex Christiansen made his further education choices, he chose physiotherapy.

Disability can, inevitably, be divisive within a family. For the Christiansens they were all in it together and that would probably never be more apparent than at Athens 2004, and not just because Sophie was about to make her debut in the biggest multi-sport event in the world for athletes with a disability.

Caroline and Karl Christiansen had loved Greece long before the Paralympic Games were a speck on their horizon. In 1980, Karl had taken up a post as deputy headmaster at TASIS Hellenic International School in Athens. Three years later Caroline, who had only recently qualified, took up a junior teaching job at the same school. It was here they met and fell in love. When their children were born they chose names that reminded them of their time abroad and would work in either language: Sophie (or Sofia) and Alex (or Alexander). In 2002, two years before the 2004 Games, they returned for a family holiday.

Walking any distance and often over uneven paths and steep inclines was too much of a challenge for Sophie, particularly around such landmarks as the Acropolis and the Parthenon. Undeterred, Karl put her on his back and hiked up the paths so all could enjoy the breathtaking views that awaited them. It was definitely worth it.

They didn't know then that two years later, they would be back for a far more emotional trip to the top. By 2004, it wasn't the ancient sights Sophie had her mind set on, she was far more focused on heading towards the summit of Paralympic Equestrian sport.

***

To spend any time with Sophie Christiansen is to know she is severely physically disabled but she is in no way mentally impaired. In fact quite the opposite, as she combines training for London 2012 with studying for an MSci in Mathematics at the Royal Holloway University of London, an achievement not lost on brother Alex. 'You can probably tell how bright she is because she's doing a Maths degree,' he says.

In terms of her disability, though, Sophie has much to contend with as she does not have complete control over any of her limbs and walks with the aid of plastic splints on her ankles and supportive footwear, all of which prevent her ankles bending inwards. When she rides, she wears boots with specially-made footwear fitted inside. She cannot complete simple tasks others might take for granted, such as putting on her shoes or tying shoe laces, without assistance as she has little fine motor coordination. If, for example, she wanted to have her ears pierced or wear contact lenses she would need a carer, or helper, to put them in and take them out every time. Nor could she balance her own body while, at the same time, holding something like a hot drink in her hand. So, against that backdrop the fact that she competes, and wins, against the best riders with a disability in the world is remarkable. As is her ability to concentrate for four and a half minutes – the approximate time it takes to complete a competition Dressage 'Test'. And although competing has physical challenges, it also brings exhilarating benefits and much-valued respite. 'With the horses it is a form of relief and allows me to get away from everyday life,' Sophie explains. 'There are things I can do on a horse that other non-disabled people can't. I am quite disabled, even though I don't see myself that way: when I am on a horse I just feel free and can forget about the difficulties of everyday life.'

One of Sophie's innate, inexplicable gifts is her ability to feel the horse beneath her and control fine movements, which create near-perfect harmony between horse and rider. It is not something you can really teach or adequately explain; it is just a skill she has. 'Her natural ability does not come from either of us,' says Karl.

'Sophie has talent, ability and knowledge,' says coach Clive Milkins. 'And the extra X factor.' And she also loves the thrill of pitting her skills against others. 'I have always liked competition,' she says. 'I think you always have to have that goal in your head. Even though I don't enjoy training and riding when it is pouring with rain, you have to think if you don't train today you might not be able to experience that fantastic feeling of winning a gold medal for your country again.'

Paralympic Equestrian consists of Dressage Tests. The Team Test and Championships Test are made up of a series of movements that must be completed within a set amount of time; the third, the Freestyle Test, involves performing a given number of movements set to music.

The only difference between the tests done by different Grades is that the most severely disabled riders – in Grades I and II – only complete movements which involve the horse walking or trotting. It is only in Grades III and IV that the horse will walk, trot and canter. In other words, the only difference in what a spectator will see is what the horse is doing.

When Christiansen arrived in Athens in 2004 there was little expectation of her. She was, after all, the youngest rider from all countries taking part. She was selected for as something of a wild card in order that when Beijing 2008 came around four years later, she would be more experienced at international level and ready for the pressure and increased expectation on her. However Sophie really didn't take too much notice. 'I have always been quite competitive,' she says. 'I want to do the best in all aspects of my life, be it sport or getting a decent degree. Even when I was little, I loved competing – it just reflects my personality.'

And so it was at the Markopoulo Equestrian Centre on a hot Athens day that Sophie Christiansen surprised everyone and took a bronze medal in her category. There have been many medals and numerous honours since, including an MBE, but this is the one they all remember, probably because of the way the story unfolded in front of them.

Luckily for the Christiansens Clare Balding was commentating for the BBC that day. Balding's father, Ian, was one of the country's leading racehorse trainers before retiring in 2002 and what his daughter doesn't know about equestrian and elite horse riding isn't worth knowing. As the competition unfolded, it was Balding who pointed out Christiansen looked to have snatched third place by the narrowest of margins. Her score flashed up – less than a point ahead of the USA's Keith Newerla who had to settle for fourth. The bronze was indeed secured.

Hearing this, Caroline struggled to keep her emotions in check. But the men in her family, meanwhile, didn't even try to hold back. 'I was in floods of tears,' Alex says. 'I was in another country watching my sister compete in a worldwide competition in front of lots of television cameras. It opened my eyes to how good she was. Up until that point I just didn't realise her talent and there I was sitting with a couple of thousand people, watching and thinking, that's my sister coming third in the world!'

Sitting next to him, Karl Christiansen was equally emotional at the realisation that they were all together for such a momentous moment. 'To be there as a family was a unique, special and wonderful moment,' he says. And pretty well everyone else was crying too, including Nicola Tustain, who had lent Sophie both her horse and her coach, Clive Milkins. Behind every successful athlete there is a tightly-knit team that feels the tension almost as much as the competitor, even though there is nothing they can do to influence the outcome.

'There was such a buzz,' says Sophie. 'Standing on the podium and seeing the Union Jack flag go up is like nothing else I have ever experienced. I think that is why I do it because not many people ever get to have that feeling in their lives.'

Suddenly she was thrust into the media spotlight and everyone wanted to talk to her about her achievement. 'I was always quite self-conscious about my speech,' she says, 'but in Athens because I won a medal, I was forced to talk to people and give interviews. When I won bronze it was one of the most special medals I have ever won – it is a moment I will never forget.'

Did the young Sophie Christiansen have the talent to make it as a Paralympic rider? Without doubt, yes. Was she committed enough to put in the huge amount of time needed to perfect her craft? Absolutely. Was she lucky enough to be in a sport which has a well-established way of spotting the next generation of medal winners and helps them realise their potential? Definitely. She also had the full backing of her family. 'My family have helped me to try and fulfill my dreams,' she says. And she also became part of a well-organised and well-run stables that had the resources and vision to take her to the very top.

By Athens 2004, Sophie Christiansen's journey from rehabilitation activity to recognition on the world stage was complete, even if her career was just beginning. As she leaned forward to receive her medal, she was half a world away another athlete, who later became friends with her, but was just beginning her own Paralympic journey.

***

Like many little girls, Helene Raynsford, who grew up non-disabled, wanted to pull on a leotard and tutu, wear pretty ballet shoes and grace the world's finest stages while completing an effortless *pas de deux* in front of sell-out audiences. Unlike most young girls, though, for Helene this was more than a dream. At 10 she entered full-time ballet school and then joined The Royal Ballet School, the world-renowned classical institution in London, aged 16.

It could have been growing up with an older sister who was in the Great Britain Synchronised Swimming team, or an innate talent, but Helene learnt about discipline and dedication at a young age. She loved the precision and excellence classical ballet offered, as well as the chance to be rhythmical and completely in tune with her body. 'I thrive in environments where I am pushed to be the best I can be,' she says, 'and ballet is all about that. You are taught as a young dancer that life at the top is performance orientated and if you don't meet the standard, you can find your schooling terminated at the end of the academic year.'

In the end it wasn't a performance failure on Raynsford's behalf that ended a promising career but an insurmountable ankle injury. At 17, the dream was over. Helene left The Royal Ballet School and returned to live with her parents in Camberley, Surrey. 'I was absolutely mad about ballet but there was no way round the injury,' she adds. 'For a while I found it hard – I couldn't watch too much ballet.' Drawing on years of hard work and application, which would later resurface in her life, Helene threw all her energies into getting good enough A-levels to study Medical Biochemistry at the Royal Holloway University of London in Egham, Surrey.

Once at Royal Holloway, she was soon fully immersed in university life, mixing work with sports activities like fencing and trampolining, although largely for the social, rather than physical, aspects. Like any 21-year-old, she was enjoying the independence and freedom university life offers.

The freedom turned out to be short-lived, however. In the summer of 2001, without warning her life turned on its head. Born with Ehlers-Danlos Syndrome, a genetic condition which leads to extremely flexible and loose joints, Helene underwent an operation, which resulted in a catastrophic brain injury. As a result she was left unable to speak, walk or take care of herself.

Remarkably, considering the severity of the injury, she recovered enough to be discharged from hospital and return home with parents, Maureen, a nurse, and Robin, an electrician, who would look after her from then on. They were advised to consider care as the only long-term option for her. There was no suggestion, or even possibility, that one day she might return to her previous life as a vivacious, outgoing young woman, they were told.

In fact, for the next eight months, from August 2001 until March 2002, Helene remembers nothing. She had no short-term memory and even simple tasks, such as picking up a knife or fork to feed herself, were beyond her grasp. 'I could speak but my sentences came out jumbled and I quite often used different words for things when I could not think of the obvious word for the item I was talking about,' she says. For example, if Helene wanted to say 'thermometer' but couldn't remember what it was called, she would say 'temperature-taker' instead.

Helene's long loss of memory and lack of awareness about the seriousness of her condition was probably, in hindsight, a saving grace.

'I think it put me in a better position psychologically than, say, someone who has a spinal injury and has the full capacity to understand what has happened,' she says.

When her speech recovered enough, she told Maureen and Robin that she wanted to return to Royal Holloway and complete her degree. Secretly shocked, they decided to go along with the plan so as not to set back her recovery. 'My mum only agreed to meet with the university to discuss the possibility that I might return because she was certain they would say no,' Helene explains.

In fact, Royal Holloway were both realistic and welcoming. Not only did they encourage Helene's return and re-integration into student life, they laid on fellow students to take her to and from lectures. 'They were fantastic. I am sure I made the progress I did because they made it possible for me to go back,' she says.

As the injury affected different parts of Helene's brain she was left with various impairments, including memory loss and a lack of motor control and feeling. So, for example, while she could turn on the shower, she couldn't tell the difference between hot and cold, or remember seismic world events like the attack on the Twin Towers in New York of September 2001.

Over time, as her feeling and memory was restored, Helene regained independence in many areas but she didn't regain control over the lower part of her body, which meant she would have to rely on a wheelchair, if not forever, at least for the foreseeable future. All of which could seem like an uphill battle and took an inevitable toll, particularly on her self-esteem. 'Having to rely so much on others had a big effect on me. People do perceive you differently when you are in a wheelchair, and because I couldn't control some of my movements and sometimes I looked a bit dazed, people treated me as if I had learning difficulties. They would frequently speak over the top of me and I lost my confidence.'

It was also a time when she found out who her friends were. There were the ones who couldn't cope and invariably, faded away and others who would go to any lengths to help her regain independence, meaning and motivation in her life. And it was one of the latter group who suggested Helene visit Variety Village in Toronto, Canada – a world-renowned centre which works with young people to help them integrate sport and life skills.

By the time the 10-day trip was over Helene Raynsford was a very different person, having tried practically every sport the Village offered, including athletics, swimming, wheelchair basketball, wheelchair fencing, rock climbing and even an aerial wheelchair assault course 40 feet up in the air. 'By the time I got home from Canada I realised I could do whatever I wanted,' she says.

Like others before her, Helene had experienced sport in a reparative way, which opened the door to participating back home. Suddenly she realised being in a wheelchair was no longer a barrier to trying the things others had said would forever be out of reach. Perhaps, though, the most liberating experience of all was being surrounded by people who made no distinction between non-disabled and disabled. 'It was eye-opening to be in an environment that was both welcoming and integrated,' she says.

Back in the UK, invigorated by the experience, Helene took up wheelchair basketball. Soon her natural ability was noticed and by

2005, she was competing for Britain at the annual Paralympic World Cup in Manchester, the biggest multi-sport competition outside the Paralympic Games. Although there were medals for Britain and Helene enjoyed the fast, physical aspects of the sport, something was lacking.

In the summer of 2005, by now working in health care, Helene had a meeting at Eton Dorney, Windsor, where the Rowing events for the Olympic and Paralympic Games will be held at London 2012. Under pressure with work deadlines and reluctant to make the journey from her office in Guildford to Windsor, she tried to get out of the meeting, to no avail. Her presence, she was told, was essential. The minute the meeting ended, she was keen to leave until a colleague persuaded her to join him on the bank to watch the rowing that was taking place. 'I'd never seen rowing in my life,' she remembers, 'and yet I couldn't help but be gripped by the buzz and excitement.'

As Helene returned to her car, interest pricked, she saw an athlete with a disability wearing a Great Britain rowing top and wondered how on earth someone without the use of their legs could perform in a sport known for its need for balance and for the strength and power required from the lower body.

Paralympic Rowing includes boats which are both single-sex and mixed gender. The sport was first introduced at the World Rowing Championships in Seville in 2002, when 38 rowers took part. It is included at London 2012 for the second time in Paralympic Games' history and has grown since it was first contested – 96 athletes are expected to participate in four medal events.

In the months that followed, Helene decided to try rowing as a way to stay fit in the build-up to the new wheelchair basketball season.

'I actually really liked it,' she recalls, 'although I was utterly useless.' She then attended to the 2005 National Championships in Nottingham and after just six months of rowing, won her category – the Arms Only Women's Single Sculls (AW1x). 'The vibe was so different from wheelchair basketball, it was exhilarating,' she says.

Her technique and experience may have been found wanting in the early days, but being in a boat gave her something she thought lost for ever. 'There are no similarities in terms of physique between a rower and a ballet dancer,' she explained, 'but in terms of attention to detail and learning how to move a boat in what appears to be a fluent, effortless and graceful way, they are very similar.'

As 2005 closed and a new year beckoned, Helene decided to set clear intentions. The World Championships were coming to Eton Dorney in 2006 and for the first time Helene's class, the Single Scull, was included. The possibility of competing at the World Championships was within her grasp.

She took a picture frame and placed it on a wall at home. In the frame was the medal won from the National Championships and then, next to it, a gap which she intended to fill with a gold medal from the World Championships. In the meantime, she placed a postcard, advertising the event at Eton Dorney, in the gap. 'Whenever I had to get up early and go training before work when it was cold and wet outside, I would look at that frame and tell myself the reason I was doing it was so I could put the gold medal in the empty space. It was a way to motivate myself.'

Whatever the psychology, the approach was devastatingly effective. Helene gained selection for the World Championships and went on to win the Single Scull Adapative Rowing title by a massive 12-second margin – the kind of margin that's almost unheard of. Britain's newest World Champion was enjoying a new lease of life. In a boat, the differences between disabled and non-disabled athletes are not immediately obvious. 'In some ways the joy of being in a rowing boat is that I'm not sitting in my chair,' she says. 'It's a step towards normality and the movement you get in a boat is liberating. I really like training in a natural environment and when I am rowing, I don't feel I am doing disability sport.'

That normality was helped by the approach taken by British Rowing, which has been highly successful in integrating the relatively new Paralympic Rowing squad into a well-established, and successful, Olympic one. This means Paralympic Rowers learn from the outset what is expected in terms of performance and behaviour, and it has positive knock-on benefits for both sets of rowers. 'One of the things that appealed to me about rowing was the way British Rowing integrate it. It's a very good system and we work as hard as an Olympic athlete,' Helene says.

And hard work was certainly what she took on in the period between winning the World Championships of 2006 and going to Beijing in 2008, where Paralympic Rowing was featuring on the Paralympic programme for the first time. Despite continuing health problems, which almost ruined her Paralympic debut, she repeated her World Championship performance and added Paralympic Gold to the World Gold now sitting in the picture frame at home.

Whatever else happens in Helene Raynsford's life she will always be the athlete who won the first-ever Rowing gold medal at the Paralympic

Games. 'No one can ever take that away from me,' she says, 'and there was huge excitement at the enormity of that achievement.'

But it wasn't until Helene and her teammates returned to the UK and took part in the joint Olympic and Paralympic parade in October 2008 that all the hard work and effort really sank in. 'It was nice to meet Gordon Brown and go to Buckingham Palace, but for all the people we got to meet it was good for them to be seen around the athletes. But the parade was on a really cold day and the streets were absolutely crammed. I remember one old lady standing on a stool by the side of the road with a huge flag: that's when I realised we really had gone out and achieved something,' she continues.

And she'll probably never forget the moment the floats had to stop and people lining the streets called out her name and shouted their congratulations. 'We had missed the build-up to the Olympics at home because we were training in Spain and until that day, we had no idea how much the nation were behind us. It gave us all such a sense of recognition,' she adds.

Helene's delight was short-lived, as she had to take 2009 off because of illness. In 2010, with eyes on London, she decided to prepare to race again. The lure of a home Games and the rapturous public reception were factors too important to ignore. 'I would love to defend my title in 2012,' she says.

For Helene, who will be 32 by the start of the London 2012 Games, it's a strong pull, not least because Eton Dorney was where she was first introduced to rowing, to an experience she will never forget and to an event that changed her life. 'As a dancer I was classed as elegant. When you have a disability, especially a movement disorder like I have, you are not classed as elegant any more. And yet when you are in the boat, the movement to push it through the water is very elegant.'

It was also the place she became the first-ever World Champion in her class and where Maureen and Robin saw their daughter once more brimming with the vitality of life. Add to that Helene Raynsford on top of the podium, a Union Flag around her shoulders and another rising to the top of the flagpole while the National Anthem drifts towards the thousands of expected spectators and it's a compelling image. And surely, that's one thing that little girls dream will happen to them when they grow up.

Chapter Five

It Could Happen to Anyone

**'Acceptance of what happens is the
first step to overcoming the
consequences of any misfortune.'**
William James, psychologist and philosopher

There are those who are born with a disability and others who are catapulted into it through traumatic accident, by being in the wrong place at the wrong time, or because of illness.

But whether it's a random incident or a genetic condition the consequences are devastating for those whose lives change in an instant. After all, how can it be that one day a tall, fit young man walks through a door and finds, a few hours later, that all use of his lower limbs has gone? How do you explain to a bright, sporty teenager that the darkness that has closed in and destroyed his vision between going to bed the night before and getting up the following morning is both irreparable and permanent? Or tell a soldier's mother that her son, whom she just waved goodbye to after being on leave, has stepped on a mine in a foreign land and had half his leg blown away?

Life, with accident, illness and malice, happens but that does not make the injustice of it any easier to accept – initially, at least. Because occasionally, those who have had their life's dreams ripped away without warning have been able to turn devastating events into huge success.

***

It was Saturday 12 February 2005 and spring term was in full swing at Warwick University. Even so, it was the weekend and Tom Aggar, a 6ft 3in, rugby-playing 21-year-old, was looking forward to kicking back and relaxing a bit. After all, life was pretty good: lectures and essays for his Biological Sciences degree were well on track and after three happy years, student life was nearing an end. What's more, unlike many young men his age, Aggar had a good idea of what he wanted to do next.

As a young boy, and throughout his time at Queen Elizabeth's School Barnet, North London, Aggar lived to play sport. He was good enough to swim and play water polo for Hertfordshire and be spotted by rugby's Saracens Youth Development squad, which he later joined. As school gave way to university, he continued to impress on the rugby field, playing second-row forward for Warwick University's First XV.

Such was his love of sport and the outdoors that he felt drawn towards a life in the military after graduation and applied to be an officer in the Royal Marines. 'I didn't think there was a bigger challenge than the Marines,' he explains. Motivated not by Britain's invasion of Iraq almost two years earlier, but by a desire to face new and bigger physical and mental challenges, Aggar had attended two interviews and subsequently been invited to a Royal Marines assessment weekend later in 2005.

In addition, he had another reason to look forward to that particular February weekend. Joe, his 19-year-old brother, was visiting from his home in Enfield, north London and as always, he knew they would enjoy spending time together. The older they got, the closer the bond between them seemed to grow.

Chapter Five

Aggar heard about a party a few miles away in Leamington at the home of one of his fellow rugby players and the brothers decided to attend. The house was at the end of a steep drive and next to it, at a much lower level, was a block of flats with a concrete drive.

It was around 8pm when they arrived at the house, which was already full to bursting. By 9pm it was so crowded Tom decided to head for a side door and into the garden to join Joe, who he'd seen going out the same way earlier in the evening. Leaving the noise and light of the house behind, he stepped outside and into an experience nothing could ever have prepared him for. He was met by complete darkness and an eerie silence: it was pitch black. Without a torch, an outside light or a brightly shining moon to illuminate the way, it was impossible to see. He took a few moments to adjust his vision and then headed towards the garden. And then he did what thousands of us have done in our lifetimes and thought nothing of: he scuffed his foot. Only in Tom's case it caused him to fall forward and down a 12-foot drop onto the concrete drive of the block of flats next door, which were at a lower level to the house. Like the path he fell off, the drive was also totally unlit.

'As I fell forward I just remember losing control,' recalls Tom, who blacked out in the fall. By the time he came round, he wondered where he was and what he was doing there. 'I knew I had been knocked out. I tried getting up but it wasn't working and at first, I couldn't work out why.' As he propped himself up on his hands he discovered the reason for his lack of mobility – an excruciating pain in his back. 'I had been a lifeguard,' he says, 'and doing biology, I knew what I had done.'

Alone, in shock and hidden from view of anyone who might have gone out to look for him, Tom sat motionless. Ten minutes passed,

Left: The idea of creating a sporting event for athletes with a disability grew quickly. Dr Ludwig Guttmann (centre), founder of the Paralympic Games, escorts the Duchess of Gloucester (right) around the sixth Stoke Mandeville Games, held in 1957.

Below: Lack of wheelchair access facilities meant that athletes going to the Rome 1960 Paralympic Games had to be loaded onto the plane using a crate and a forklift truck.

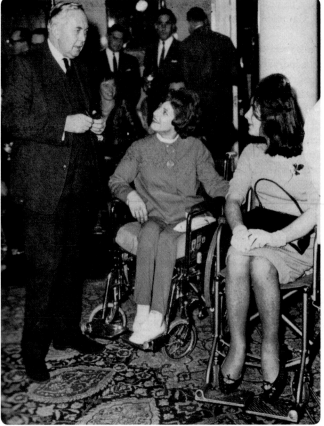

Above: British athletes on their way to the Tokyo 1964 Games. Paralympic sport was opening up a range of possibilities, such as international travel, denied to previous generations of disabled people.

Left: Even in the early days of Paralympic sport there was high-level recognition of athletes' achievements. Here, former Prime Minister Harold Wilson hosts a reception at No. 10 Downing Street in 1964.

By the 1970s, disability sport was turning into elite athlete sport, regardless of disability. Here, Philip Craven puts in some of the endless hours of practice that led him to become one of the best wheelchair basketball players in the world.

Above: Tanni Grey-Thompson arrives on the world stage with four golds and one silver at the Barcelona 1992 Games. She became one of the most decorated athletes of all time.

Below: Swimmer David Roberts is greeted by former Sports Minister Kate Hoey at Heathrow Airport, as he shows off his haul of seven medals from the Sydney 2000 Games.

Above: Sophie Christiansen at Athens 2004 with her bronze medal, trainer Clive Milkins and Charlie Girl, the horse on which she trained and which was borrowed by the Brazilian team.

Right: Lee Pearson cements his place as one of the greatest equestrian riders of all time with a gold medal in Freestyle Test: Individual – Grade 1b, at the Beijing 2008 Games. Pearson has won nine gold medals to date from nine events – a 100 per cent record.

Below: Tom Aggar's journey to become a Single Sculls – ASM1x gold-medallist at the Beijing 2008 Games took just over two years from his first experience in an adaptive racing boat.

Opposite, bottom: Archer Danielle Brown releases an arrow on her way to winning the Individual Compound – Open event at Beijing 2008. The nature of her sport means she regularly competes against non-disabled archers.

Above: Peter Norfolk wins gold at Beijing 2008. Norfolk was Britain's first gold medallist in Wheelchair Tennis, when he won the Singles – Quad competition at Athens 2004.

Helene Raynsford in training for the Single Sculls – ASW1x at Beijing 2008, an event she went on to win. Her training is integrated with non-disabled Olympic rowers.

Above: Jody Cundy competes in the Kilo at the Beijing 2008 Games. He broke the world record on his way to gold. Cundy was a former gold-medal winning swimmer.

Right: Like Jody Cundy (above) Sarah Storey was a former highly successful swimmer. Her two gold medals in Cycling at Beijing 2008 made her transition between the two sports appear effortless.

Above: Ellie Simmonds receives her MBE from the Queen in 2009. At the Beijing 2008 Games, she was the youngest British athlete at just 13 years old, but won two gold medals at 100m and 400m Freestyle – S6. She was then voted 2008 Young Sports Personality of the Year.

then another and then another. One hour became two and still he sat in silence even though help was close at hand and he could easily have accessed it. Despite the impact of the fall he had in his trouser pocket a fully charged, undamaged mobile phone with more than enough reception to make a call. But as the night wore on and sleet started to fall on the thin jumper he was wearing, the phone stayed in his pocket.

Deep down he knew. Having studied Biological Sciences for the best part of three years, been a lifeguard and completed First Aid courses, he had a better understanding than most about the way the body moves and how it works. The pain he was in and a lack of lower-limb movement enabled him to make an educated guess about his injury, but, initially at least, shock and denial set in and he needed time alone. So he waited. 'I didn't want to call for help,' he explains, 'as then I would have to accept something pretty bad had happened.'

Eventually, more than two hours after the fall and by now freezing cold, Tom pulled out the phone and slowly tapped in 999. Calmly he told the operator what he thought he had done and where the crew could find him. The place where he fell wasn't visible from the road so at first the ambulance drove right past, forcing him to call back to direct them. He still hadn't told anyone in the house what had happened.

As the paramedics arrived Tom told them what he thought he had done. They placed him on a spinal board before making the short trip to Coventry Hospital. Once there he was taken for a CT scan which would, in time, confirm what he himself suspected, although no information was revealed. The scans showed beyond doubt that his lower back was broken and he was paralysed from the waist down.

As nurses and doctors came and went they repeatedly asked permission to call his parents who, along with Joe, remained unaware of unfolding events. For Joe, the youngest person affected by events that night, the aftermath was devastating. Having looked for his brother for ages and having failing to find him, he decided to head back to the Warwick campus alone, fully expecting to find Tom already in his room waiting for him.

But Aggar was in Coventry Hospital and, despite the shock and pain, still refused each request to contact Joe, or Marion and Bob, his parents. By now it was late on Saturday night and in all likelihood his parents would already be asleep at the family home he and Joe had grown up in.

He wanted to afford them one more night of thinking their bright, talented, fit son was on the verge of finishing his degree and about to embark on a post-university selection course, which, if successful, would see him join the Royal Marines. What possible good would be served by having a total stranger call his sleeping parents in the middle of the night with the sort of devastating news that would forever change all their lives? 'I just could not imagine them getting that news,' says Tom.

Not so long ago it was young men of Tom Aggar's age who were most at risk of sustaining a spinal-cord injury. Car and motorbike crashes were the likely cause, followed by sporting accidents, but today it's a different story.

Improvements in car and motorbike safety, as well as more advanced roadside treatment following collisions means paralysis is more likely to come from falls, such as the one Tom had, from ladders, trees or heights, than from traffic accidents. The number of incidences of paralysis from sporting accidents, such as diving into shallow water, falling from a horse or playing rugby remains relatively small. A more active population later in life brings its own risks as a greater number of older people sustain serious spinal-cord injuries, usually as a result of a fall. According to the Spinal Injuries Association (SIA), three quarters of spinal injuries occur to men with an average age nearer to 40 than 20.

Definitive statistics, though, remain hard to come by. Much like the history of the Paralympics themselves, accurate data is scarce and difficult to corroborate. This is partly because spinal cord injuries are not defined as a 'notifiable disease or condition' by the Government and so hospitals are under no obligation to keep such statistics and partly because those who do keep statistics are the specialist spinal cord centres to which patients are often transferred, from a general hospital following an accident. But not all patients go down this route and those who are not transferred are, as a result, omitted from the data.

According to the Spinal Injuries Association (SIA), anywhere between 800 and 1,200 people will have a spinal injury each year in the UK. This takes the number of spinally injured to between 35,000 and 40,000 – still a relatively small number compared to those affected by strokes or cancer in the UK. Unlike stroke or cancer sufferers, though, those confined to a wheelchair are likely to live with the condition for a very long time, particularly as improvements in medicine and living conditions enhance life expectancy.

When a spinal-cord injury occurs the messages that travel through the spinal cord to the brain are impaired. These messages can either be completely or partially cut off. An incomplete injury will result in some function below the level of the injury, although this function may be compromised. A complete injury is where all sensation and muscle control is lost below the level of the injury. Nearly half of all spinal cord injuries are complete.

***

Back in Coventry Hospital, Tom Aggar finally conceded. Night had given way to day and he agreed to let the hospital contact his parents knowing, in many ways, the news would be even harder on them than it was on him.

The call Marion and Bob received in London that morning would tell them only that their son had been involved in an accident in which he had hurt his neck and that they should come immediately. The two-hour journey north must have seemed never-ending.

Whatever fears they had were confirmed as they pulled into the hospital car park. There to greet them was a party of nurses and the surgeon in charge of Tom's care. It didn't take long to realise the presence of a surgeon, so early on a Sunday morning, could only mean the prognosis was not good. As they made their way inside there was more distressing news to come. A young nurse grabbed Marion by the arm, explaining Tom would never walk again and told her to prepare herself, and her family, for what lay ahead.

For Marion, grappling with her own shock and denial, it was far too much information to absorb in one go, particularly as neither she nor Bob had any medical background or expertise. 'As a parent you expect them to crash your car or have to be picked up when they are out late and drunk but this was totally out of our framework as parents and I remember thinking, I don't know how to deal with this,' Marion now recalls.

When the consultant showed her the scan of Tom's back and the point at which it was broken he explained the back was very badly swollen as a result of the traumatic impact. Surely, Marion reasoned, if the injury was recent and swollen and it was given time to settle, recovery would follow? After all, broken bones, even in the back, will heal.

But not this particular bone, and not in Tom's back. As the chat with the surgeon came to an end, Marion and Bob faced the first of many agonising decisions. Would they, or the surgeon, tell Tom the heartbreaking news?

After some discussion it was felt best if the surgeon did this and so, with Bob at her side, Marion stood in the background as Tom was told he would never walk again. Less than 24 hours had passed since the fall. All Tom's parents could do was to hold each other's hands, hearts aching, and know that whatever abyss Tom had fallen into the night before, they would be there for him as they all began their own journeys into the unknown.

In the days that followed Tom faced a choice: lie in bed for three months and rest to allow his damaged back to heal or opt for an operation to fuse and stabilise the back, above and below the break. He chose the latter and was soon moved to Stanmore, close to his parents' home, where the procedure and his subsequent rehabilitation could take place.

Once Tom had recovered from surgery, he began the long and slow, frustrating journey into a new, unplanned life. 'At first I was in so much pain I just had to lie and look at the ceiling. I tried not to get frustrated: you can throw a tantrum or just get on with it. Even so, there were horrible times when I just wanted to have a shower and wash my hair – you just have to deal with it.'

If it was hard for Tom, he was at least in the early days cushioned by morphine and the fact that he didn't accept the injury was permanent. 'I thought I would recover and I did have that belief for the first six weeks. I was so fit and strong, if anyone had a good chance of recovery it was me,' he explains.

For Marion and Bob, forced to watch from the sidelines, there was no denial only the dawning realisation that there was nothing, practically, they could do but offer constant love and support, and in Marion's case, a stream of home-cooked meals to alleviate the boredom of hospital food. 'If you see your child struggle, it is the worst thing in the world,' she says, 'and it doesn't get any easier.'

While Tom's days were filled with various activities, such as learning the basic skills of getting in and out of a wheelchair unaided and then manoeuvring his new mode of transport in and out of the tightest spaces, his parents could do no more but sit and watch. 'It was almost harder for them,' Tom recalls. 'There really was nothing they could do.' Things came to a head one day when, during a visit, Marion and Bob just sat and stared. In the end Tom had to ask them what they were staring at. 'I think it was just their shock and frustration,' he says.

Sometimes that frustration would be turned into action and Marion would spend hours on the hospital's internet service searching for information or an insight into some new miracle cure that might lead to a change in her son's long-term physical outlook. Until one day when one of the doctors gave her a piece of advice she would never forget: 'Don't use your energy to search – use it all to go forward.'

From that moment onwards Marion realised there was no point in looking back to possible, yet-to-be discovered medical solutions: she needed to look to Tom's future, albeit now different to the one she might have imagined. 'In my naivety I've always been able to help my children but in this case it wasn't possible,' she says, 'there was no answer.'

So instead she used her energy to re-focus, to change direction and think what Tom might do with his life next, what kind of wheelchair he needed and how he could be more independent. And so they looked forward, not back.

Like all parents who find their lives irreversibly changed by a random, inexplicable event, Marion had to come to terms with the fact that this was something over which she had no control. 'I couldn't put it right,' she says. 'You stand up for them at school to make sure they don't get bullied, you take them to the GP to get them the right inoculations and you put every part of your being into making sure you do the best for them, and then this evil thing happened and there was nothing I could do. I couldn't resolve it: I was so mad about it.'

As the weeks in Stanmore passed there were two people now involved in the lives of the Aggar family, who saw the kind of struggle they faced and knew exactly what to do. Occupational therapist Lynne Hills and physiotherapist Tania Smith worked to restore some of the basic skills needed in everyday life. Tom had been placed in a plastic cast from his hips to his underarms to help his spine heal correctly: any kind of movement was hard and challenging, and his legs were heavy weights which he had to lift from one place and put down in another.

'You are lying in bed wondering how to put your life back together,' says Tom. 'It was the approach of Lynne and Tania that was such an eye-opener. After I spent time with them, I worked hard and got on with it. They teach you how to dress and how to get in and out of bed. They are the little things you take for granted, but they are also the things that make you independent: they are showing you your way back into life.'

Just weeks into a three-month hospital stay, Tania Smith made a prediction. 'One day,' she said, 'Tom Aggar will go to the Paralympic Games.' Aggar laughed the suggestion off and yet one key quality remained undimmed by the accident, which she had perhaps seen. His competitive spirit was very much alive. Six weeks after surgery, complete with a stiff, plastic body brace to protect his fused spine and ensure it healed in a straight position, Tom wheeled himself into Stanmore's hospital gym and started to improve his strength and fitness, still believing if a cure to paralysis could be found through stem cell development then the fitter he was, the more chance he would have of benefiting. 'In the early days I did think I would recover. It gave me the motivation to get back on track. It wasn't about getting in shape to compete, it was about being fit to be ready, if a medical breakthrough came,' he explained.

By May 2005, he was well enough to go home and then decided to return to Warwick to finish his degree. The University was magnificent, providing a ground-floor flat, wet room and disabled parking bay, while his fellow students, who had never known him before the accident, readily pitched in to help whenever needed. Sociable and affable by nature, Tom had no difficulty in making friends.

And so it was with immense pride that Marion, Bob and Joe were on hand to see Tom graduate with a First in the summer of 2006. A bit later than originally planned perhaps, but mission nonetheless more than accomplished.

***

By then pretty fit from swimming and gym workouts, Aggar already knew about a new type of rowing machine for the disabled from his time at Stanmore. This was a pioneering type of rower for those unable to use their legs, which artificially stimulated the muscles in a similar way to a non-disabled person. Tom decided to have a go and immediately loved it. He then entered himself in the British Indoor Rowing Championships and duly won his category in a new world record time.

It was here that he came into contact with the Paralympic squad and by late 2006, tried rowing on the water for the first time at East London's Royal Docks: 'My goal then was not to compete at the Paralympic Games, but to enjoy it.' And it was a goal he more than met. 'There was no part I didn't enjoy,' he recalls. 'Psychologically, it gets you out of the chair. You are forced to spend 12 hours a day in it, not by choice. Initially, it gave me such a sense of freedom. For a while I did resent being resigned to moving around in a chair and rowing was a way to get out of it.'

Although he could not steer particularly well and his university-acquired fitness proved meagre against the endurance of other rowers, Tom had the bug. And, despite a lack of elite level fitness, he quickly proved good at the sport.

By March 2007, he was winning the men's Single Sculls at the British selection trials for the World Championships in Munich later that year, and by the summer of 2007 he beat the reigning World Champion, setting a new Paralympic record at the same time. 'Going to Munich opened my eyes up to the sport and how everyone else in the world was training. Getting selected to represent Great Britain was brilliant. I got such a buzz from the competition, knowing I was competing in the sport at the very highest level,' he says.

Next stop Beijing 2008, and Tom Aggar couldn't wait. He wanted to be in the best shape possible. Not, this time, in case of some new development in stem cell research: he now had a very different goal. He wasn't about to dedicate the next year of his life to come second – he was going to Beijing to win.

If Tom thought he had trained hard in the run-up to the 2007 World Championships, he was in for a bit of a shock. As 2007 ended and the banks of the River Thames lit up in a blaze of fireworks to welcome in 2008, members of the British Paralympic Rowing squad were about to get a boost of their own as training and preparation reached new levels of intensity.

Back in 1960, when the very first Games for the Paralysed were held outside the UK, there had been a call, even then, to add new events to the programme. The Paralympic Games of the 21st century are no different as athletes, International Federations and countries all clamour to have new sports added. At the next Games after London 2012, the Rio de Janeiro 2016 Paralympic Games, Para-Triathlon and Para Canoe will take the existing number of sports from 20 to 22.

At Beijing 2008, the new sport on the block was Rowing and suddenly everyone was taking it a lot more seriously. Rowing – where the equipment is adapted to the disability of the competitor, and the distance shortened from the 2000m used at Olympic regattas to 1000m

– was about to make its Paralympic debut. 'I thought training five or six times a week was a lot. Now it was three times a day, just like the Olympic squad,' says Aggar. 'I had never been in a set-up which was pushing you as an athlete.'

And although Aggar and the rest of the squad were still training in Spain when the Olympic Games took place, watching teammates like Zac Purchase and Mark Hunter power to victory on the same lake the Paralympic team would be competing on in a few weeks' time only served to motivate and inspire them through the last days of training. As would the knowledge that whatever training the British Olympic team had done, the Paralympic approach had been similarly methodical and thought through.

Back in London Marion, Bob and Joe Aggar were making plans of their own, preparing to fly to Beijing to watch Tom in action. They wouldn't miss this moment for the world.

At the Shunyi Olympic Rowing-Canoeing Park in Beijing Aggar progressed to the final of the men's Single Sculls without incident and returned to the Village to make his final preparations.

In another part of Beijing, Marion was also preparing for the next day and wondering how she would console her son if he did not win. As she settled down, sleep proved elusive and she spent a good part of it lying awake. 'I just wanted to get there and take my seat in the stands,' she says.

When the big day finally came, Tom needed to prepare physically and mentally. He pushed his chair ever quicker around the lake to warm up and then stretched every muscle. All the time he was plugged into his MP3 player, listening to rapper Eminem.

Unaware of the pre-race rituals Tom was going through, Marion and the rest of the Aggar family were busy taking their seats and making friends with the Americans and Canadians sitting nearby. Back in Barnet, north London pupils at Tom's old school, Queen Elizabeth's, gathered round the television and waited.

As the moments ticked by, Marion could only sit and hope the final preparations had gone to plan and that all the rigging and strapping – required to hold the rowers in a fixed position so as to avoid falling forward during the race – was in place. 'If Tom knew, he would think I was mad but I was just willing everything to be perfect for him,' she says.

As it turned out, as races go at this level it was pretty faultless. Slightly ahead of the Ukrainian rower, Oleksandr Petrenko at the 500m, or halfway point, Aggar began to pull away. By the 750m point his boat cut a graceful sight as his superior strength meant each stroke took him closer to the finishing line and gold.

'I knew it was in the bag,' said Marion, while not underestimating the physical pain Tom would be in as the build-up of lactic acid in his arms screamed for him to stop. Minutes later, amid a cacophony of noise which drowned everything else out, Aggar crossed the line as Britain's first-ever men's Paralympic Rowing champion.

Up in the stands Marion hugged and kissed Bob, who hugged Joe, who found himself embraced by total strangers. All around British flags waved as a jubilant contingent of friends, family and supporters clapped and cheered with delight.

Every parent will tell you they can spot their child a mile off. For most, it will be as they run out onto the pitch for football practice or meander out of the school gates at the end of the day. For a tiny minority, it will be when witnessing their child doing something extraordinary. Marion and Bob Aggar were about to join that elite club as Tom wheeled towards the victory podium. 'I could see this beautiful, smiling face,' Marion says. Tom bent his head to receive the ultimate sporting accolade, a Paralympic gold medal. As he lifted a British flag and savoured the moment not for the first time in recent years his parents could not quite believe what they saw, although this time their disbelief was accompanied by different emotions.

'He deserved it,' says Marion. 'Not because he had an accident but because he had put his heart and soul into it. As a mother, I had the best possible outcome from something so awful happening.'

Meanwhile, amid the euphoria congratulatory hugs, kisses and the camaraderie and support from teammates, Tom Aggar's phone lit up with calls and congratulatory text messages. 'Well done on winning gold. If I'm not mistaken a certain person predicted you would be in the Paralympic Games one day. Congratulations!' bleeped one. Not recognising the number, he scrolled down to see who it was from.

Few could have believed a journey that began with an unfathomable accident on a garden path more than three years earlier would alight here, on the outskirts of China's capital city on a sunny autumnal day in front of thousands of cheering Chinese and an ecstatic British rowing camp. Among those who did see the possibilities and opportunities that lay ahead for the young man before her was the sender of this particular text. And her name? Tania Smith from Stanmore hospital's physiotherapy department.

***

Paralysis caused by accident becomes even more difficult to deal with when the cause is beyond your own control and is wrapped up in great tragedy, as was the case with Josie Pearson, and her then boyfriend, Daniel Evans.

Like many young men his age, 19-year-old Daniel loved driving fast and once told Josie, two years his junior, he might well end up dead in a car accident. Born in Bristol and brought up near Hay-on-Wye, Josie didn't pay his prediction too much attention. It was 2003 and the 17-year-old was too busy riding, a sport she had fallen in love with after she first tried it at the age of four.

By the time she was 17 she had her own horse, George, to look after, train and prepare for the county competitions in cross country, dressage and show jumping, which she would regularly take part in. Riding every day was both her passion and her life, so much so she once told a friend if she could not ride, she would rather die.

And then in the summer of 2003 Josie, Daniel and three other friends were on a night out when their vehicle was involved in a fatal three-car pile-up. Daniel died instantly while Josie's best friend, Laura Miles (who was sitting next to Josie in the back) broke her pelvis and suffered internal injuries. Of the two other friends, one remarkably escaped unharmed while the other, Dan's best friend, broke his back but was not paralysed.

Josie was not so lucky, breaking her neck at level C6/C7 as the vertebrae pushed into her spinal cord, causing irreparable nerve damage and paralysis from the chest down. During her rehabilitation at Oswestry Spinal Unit, she came across a Great Britain Wheelchair Rugby player, Alan Ash, who suggested she should come along and give the sport a try. Interestingly, at Paralympic level, Wheelchair Rugby is a mixed sport made up of teams of 12 men and women, of which only four can be on court at any one time.

Initially, Josie wanted to return to riding, but when she found it neither as fulfilling or exciting as she had before her accident, she decided to take up the wheelchair rugby idea, emailing the secretary at Cardiff Pirates for information.

She enjoyed the fast and furious pace of the sport and being the only girl at Cardiff hardly mattered: she loved being part of a team and quickly proved good enough to be considered for the Great Britain squad. Eventually at the age of 22, she became the first woman to represent her country at the Beijing 2008 Paralympic Games, where the team came fourth. 'It was the most amazing experience of my life so far,' she said. 'My aim had been to represent London in 2012, so going to Beijing in the first place was so exciting.'

And yet, despite the thrill of competing, Josie missed the individuality that being solely in charge of a horse brings. The year before the Beijing Games she had tried some wheelchair track racing. 'It was like riding again,' she said. 'It really appealed to me.' Even so, it seemed far too much of a risk to change sports in the run-up to Beijing, so Pearson decided to wait, although the thought of competing on the track rather than with a rugby ball never went away.

And then in 2010 an opportunity presented itself that was too good to miss. ParalympicsGB — the governing body for Paralympic athletes in Great Britain — operates a Talent Transfer Scheme for those athletes who wish to switch from one sport to another. When Pearson met up with Peter Eriksson, who was appointed UK Athletics Paralympic Head

Coach in December 2008, he offered to coach her for 2012. Eriksson, a former international speed skater, is one of the most successful and respected, coaches in the world, having helped athletes bring home some 119 medals in seven Games, from 1984 to 2008.

He also coached the exceptional Canadian wheelchair track athlete, Chantal Petitclerc, who having lost both her legs at the age of 13 following an accident, went on to win 21 Paralympic medals in five Games, from Barcelona in 1992 to Beijing in 2008, when she retired. At Beijing 2008 she dominated the track, winning five gold medals in the 100m, 200m, 400m, 800m and 1500m, and set three world records.

It was too good an opportunity to miss. 'It was brilliant,' said Pearson. 'He knows what he is doing; he is a leader. And we get on really well.'

Inevitably the transition from a team environment to an individual one took some adjustment. 'Initially it was strange because I was so used to being surrounded by a team,' she explains, 'but I knew it was the right thing and I've never regretted it.'

Pearson was selected to race in her first major event, the IPC World Athletics Championships, in New Zealand in January 2011, and is now focused on London 2012.

Although Olympians who have switched sports, such as Rebecca Romero, who won a silver medal in the Quadruple Sculls for Britain in Rowing at Athens in 2004 and then switched to Track Cycling, winning gold in the Individual Pursuit at Beijing four years later, are extremely rare, this is not the case in Paralympic sport. If successfully selected for London 2012, Josie Pearson will join a long list of competitors who have successfully switched sports at the highest level, including Sarah

Storey (Swimming and Cycling), Jody Cundy (Swimming and Cycling) and Richard Whitehead (Ice Sledge Hockey and Athletics).

At London 2012 Pearson intends to drop the ball and concentrate instead on the 100m, 200m and 400m on the track.

***

Sometimes it is an inexplicable accident that propels the person affected into a life they or their loved ones never imagined, as was the case with Tom Aggar and Josie Pearson. Other times a cruel twist of fate has the same effect, which is what happened to 14-year-old Chris Holmes.

Born in Peterborough, Chris and his family moved at the age of three to Kidderminster, Worcestershire, where he grew up. Educated at the local comprehensive, Harry Cheshire High School, it was obvious he had a natural aptitude for sport. It was in the swimming pool he excelled and where his parents, Margaret, a part-time bookkeeper at the local cattle market, and Michael, who worked for the County Council, would happily take him to and from training.

Unlike most 14-year-olds, though, Chris went to bed one night and woke the following day to find he was almost totally blind. What little sight remained eventually also disappeared as the result of a condition called Familial Exudative Vitreoretinopathy, or FEVR. The disease varies both in intensity and effect, but in Chris's case the folds in his retina failed to grow in the usual way and instead tore, which caused at first partial and then total blindness. Although genetic, there was no history of sight problems in the family background, which meant his blindness came as a bolt from the blue.

Today Chris Holmes is one of around 370,000 people registered blind or partially sighted in this country according to figures released by the Royal National Institute of Blind People (RNID).

Losing sight permanently and unexpectedly would be difficult enough for any young teenager, let alone one with a gift for swimming and a burning desire to be good enough to compete for his country. Supported by his parents, two elder siblings, and his school, Chris made it clear that with or without his sight he still intended to swim for Britain and achieve good enough A-level grades to read Politics at Cambridge. 'It changed the practicalities but the fundamental approach remained the same,' he explains.

Three months after going blind, he was back in the pool training alongside his sighted teammates. A year later, he travelled to the Junior European Championships in Moscow, where he was well and truly beaten by better swimmers. It wasn't an experience he enjoyed, or a performance he was happy with, so Holmes decided to employ the same training methods as Olympic athletes and to do that, he needed to up his game, change to a different swimming club further from his home and adopt an entirely new mental approach to his desire for success. 'The Europeans were a real baptism of fire for me as I realised, for the first time, how hard it was going to be to be a world-class swimmer, so I had to ask myself what I needed to do to take my swimming to another level,' he says.

By the following year, less than two years after darkness had descended, Chris Holmes was on a plane to South Korea for the Seoul 1988 Paralympic Games, the first of four he would leave his mark on. This was only the fourth time blind athletes had competed at the

Paralympic Games since their inclusion, for the first time, at Toronto 1976, then at Arnhem 1980, and New York and Stoke Mandeville (the year the Games were split between two countries) in 1984.

More than any of the other Games Holmes attended, it was Seoul which forever changed his outlook, goals and ambitions. It was his first Games and as he stepped off the first-ever long-haul flight of his life, he suddenly found himself rubbing shoulders with thousands of athletes who had travelled from a hundred countries across the globe. There, he met other swimmers, archers, shooters and blind football and judo players from different cultures and backgrounds, with vastly different experiences of disability. It expanded his horizons and ambitions in a way nothing had ever done before: it would be an experience he would carry with him throughout his career and into retirement. 'I was just a boy from Kidderminster,' he says. 'We never went abroad on foreign holidays and to find myself on the other side of the world, in South Korea, was extraordinary.'

Many say it was the Seoul 1988 Games which marked a sea-change in attitudes towards Paralympic sport. From this moment on, the Paralympic Games have always been held in the same Host City as the Olympic Games and this new parity was profound. Those athletes who did compete in 1988 were overwhelmed by the experience of using exactly the same gleaming facilities the Olympians had a few weeks earlier. 'To be swimming in the pool that had just been used by the Olympians was fantastic,' says Holmes.

Returning with two silver medals and a bronze, Chris knew what he now needed to do if he wanted to be the best in the world by the time Barcelona came round in under four years' time. And that, together with successfully gaining entry to Cambridge, was the plan he put into action with spectacular results.

Chris Holmes went on to become one of the most successful British Paralympians of all time, winning nine gold medals in the pool in a career spanning 14 years. This included six gold medals in a single Paralympic Games (Barcelona 1992), a feat which, to date, has never been equalled by another British Paralympic athlete.

After retiring in 2002 following a short career working in commercial law, Holmes accepted a post as Director of Paralympic Integration at the London Organising Committee of the Olympic and Paralympic Games. His job is to ensure every aspect of the Paralympic Games is embedded in the ethos of the organising committee in a way which has never been done before. That means whether it's the food being served in the Athletes' Village or the way athletes are transported from Village to venue, the needs of the Paralympians must be as much a part of the planning as those of the Olympians.

If successful, this legacy, while considerably less visible than the sell-out crowds, church congregations and screaming schoolchildren seen in South Korea, will remain one of London's biggest and most far-reaching gifts to the Paralympic Movement.

***

But for a cruel twist of fate neither Chris Holmes nor Tom Aggar would have ended up as Paralympic athletes, let alone the best in the world at what they do. Their route to the top of the Paralympic podium came about through illness and accident respectively. And while both categories are represented at the Paralympic Games so too is another, unrelated group of athletes – those who are struck down by war.

Right from the beginning war has had a major impact on Paralympic sport. It was the fear of an influx of casualties from the push on the Second Front in spring 1944 which led to a special spinal unit being opened at Stoke Mandeville Hospital and it was ex-servicemen who took part in the first disabled competition in 1948.

Today Britain's involvement in Afghanistan has seen more than 360 soldiers die so far, a figure that will be out of date from almost the moment it is written. In addition, according to figures released by the Ministry of Defence (MOD) from 7 October 2001 when data began until 31 January 2011, 1,608 soldiers were wounded in battle. Of those the greatest number of casualties occurred in 2009 and 2010, when a total of 1,026 soldiers were wounded.

These figures show that while there has been significant loss of life from war, a large, remaining issue is the repatriation, recovery and rehabilitation of the hundreds who now survive, albeit often with horrific and life-changing injuries. Thanks to improvements in medicine and the quality of the British field hospitals in theatres of war – according to the MOD in 2010 alone there were 76 amputations.

With an ever-increasing number of wounded and maimed military personnel to account for and take care of, a military initiative called 'Battle Back' was launched on 28 July 2008, 60 years after Ludwig Guttmann started the Stoke Mandeville Games with two teams of ex-service personnel participating in Archery.

Battle Back was formed by Lieutenant Colonel Fred Hargreaves with backing from the Help for Heroes charity and £50,000 from the

Defence budget. 'There wasn't anything in place like this before,' he explained. 'Until now, some wounded Service personnel have managed to arrange their own activities through existing programmes, but there has never been a sort of "bespoke" nature to it.'

Major Martin Colclough was the first officer appointed to run the programme from Headley Court (the Defence Medical Rehabilitation Centre, near Epsom in Surrey) and was instrumental in providing a single point of contact for wounded personnel.

Although soldiers fighting in Afghanistan are more likely to step on an embedded IED (Improvised Explosive Device) and have one or both legs blown off rather than end up paralysed, the principles of Battle Back hold true to Guttmann's. The aim is to use adventure training, and sport, be that skiing in Bavaria, sitting volleyball, gliding, swimming the Channel, athletics, cycling or sailing, as an integral part of the soldiers' rehabilitation and to help them return to an independent, active life.

Battle Back is open to all servicemen and women regardless of how they have sustained their injuries. It is based in Headley Court and other Service rehabilitation centres. As well as facilitating adventure training and opportunities to play and participate in sport for all wounded personnel, Battle Back also seeks to provide access to elite sporting opportunities through various talent-identification programmes run both by National Governing Bodies (NGBs) and by ParalympicsGB.

When the London 2012 Olympics Opening Ceremony takes place on 27 July, it will be the eve of Battle Back's fourth anniversary. To date three 'Battle Backers', as they are known, have represented Britain in various sports. All are training with, and in contention for, the ParalympicsGB 2012 team. More than 24 others are active in winter

Paralympic sports. Currently, there are more elite winter Battle Backers than summer ones, with three skiers and four ice-sledge hockey players representing Britain in 2011; another has represented England in Blind Football.

One serving soldier who has benefited from the Battle Back initiative is Corporal Terry 'Tel' Byrne. Byrne only ever wanted to do one thing and that was to join the Army. Not just any old regiment, though: he wanted to be part of the elite Parachute Regiment. Whether that was because he was surrounded by five sisters growing up in Thornton-Cleveleys, near Blackpool, or he simply wanted to be the best of the best, the 26-year-old had his mind made up from the age of 12 when he told his mum, Sue (who worked in the local laundry) of his decision.

At 17, having been something of a tearaway at school who got by academically with the minimum GCSEs required, he joined up. Twenty-six weeks later, with training at Catterick, North Yorkshire, successfully completed, Tel Byrne arrived at his battalion. Days later, on his 18th birthday, he was deployed on his first tour of duty: to Northern Ireland. 'It was just miles and miles of patrolling,' he says. 'It wasn't particularly exciting, but it was a good way to join the battalion.'

Overseas exercises in the USA and Africa, and two peacekeeping tours in Iraq followed. He enjoyed every one of the challenges thrown at him. 'I loved it: I got to travel the world with my mates. The job, the training, the comradeship, I loved the whole lot of it. The mates you get in the Army, you will never get in Civvy Street,' he says. 'You are a lot closer because some of the stuff you have done together is a lot more extreme.'

By the age of 24 he'd found each tour had given him the chance to put into practice what he had learnt. 'I loved being on tour because that is what you join the Army for,' he says. 'That is when you get to work together as a team, that is when you shine as an individual, as a battalion, as a company.'

In April 2008, he was posted to Afghanistan. The days were long, up to 16 hours, and the work dangerous and demanding, often involving prolonged engagements with the enemy. But he relished the life, the chance to keep the enemy firmly on the back foot and the additional responsibility he had for the 20 or so men in his platoon. Once the day's work was done, and the kit checked and prepared for its next use, he liked nothing better than a game of chess or volleyball with his mates as a way of relaxing back at camp. 'It is hard work,' he says, 'but you also have a laugh with the blokes.'

After three months Byrne was back home in the UK for two weeks of enjoyable rest and recovery before he flew back to Afghanistan. It was 10 August 2008, two days after the Opening Ceremony of the Beijing Olympic Games.

On his first night back on duty he left his base on a 10km foot patrol at 2am with around 20 men. They would complete the patrol and then return to base. In front was a lead man, then Byrne, followed by the rest of the men. They were less than 500m from base when the group entered a field. The lead man stepped into a ditch and stepped out, Byrne stepped in and was blown out. He landed on the ground.

'I heard a massive bang and I could smell explosives burning all around me. I didn't know it was me at the time,' he says. 'I shouted, "Medic!"', instinctively knowing someone nearby needed attention. Only as he stood up and his right leg crumbled beneath him, did he realise that someone was himself. Reaching for his emergency medical supplies he gave himself a morphine injection and as he did so, realised that his little finger was badly mangled. With a doctor among his party he was stretchered back to the camp they'd just left. Less than half an hour later, he was in a helicopter on the way to Camp Bastion, the main military base for the British Army in Afghanistan, and to a fully equipped field hospital.

As Corporal Byrne was off-loaded from the helicopter he was greeted by a phalanx of doctors, nurses and surgeons, who cleaned his wounds and stablised his leg. Then he was handed a phone and asked if he would like to call his mother as it would be better for her to hear the news of his injuries from him than anyone else. After 12 hours, he was on a flight back to the UK and, less than 24 hours after being blown up, in Selly Oak Hospital, Birmingham (the Royal Centre for Defence Medicine). 'The casualty evacuation is brilliant,' he says.

After five days in Selly Oak and daily operations to try and save the little finger of his right hand, Byrne was visited by a doctor who told him his leg was very badly damaged and although they could save it, if they did so he would never walk properly again and it would have to be fused at the ankle. He recommended the leg and little finger be amputated. 'There and then, I said, "Cut it off,"' Byrne recalls. 'I was right in my own head. Everything was okay and I was quite happy about it: I knew I would get myself a fake leg and be up and running about.'

It was Wednesday 20 August. Three days earlier, at Beijing 2008, Michael Phelps secured gold in the 4 x 100m Medley Relay, taking his gold medal tally from Athens 2004 and Beijing 2008 to 14, making him the most-decorated Olympic gold medal winner of all time. On the morning of Thursday 21 August Byrne had his right leg below, the

knee and the little finger of his right hand amputated. His recovery at
Selly Oak continued for another five weeks, with him passing the time
working as hard as he could on his physiotherapy and watching the
Beijing Paralympic Games. He knew he would never be able to return
to frontline soldiering.

As he watched Britain's Paralympic cyclists, such as Jody Cundy and
Sarah Storey, power their way to victory in Beijing, he made a decision
about what he would do next. 'I said to the nurses, right, I will be there
in London,' he recalls. 'I chose there and then that was what I wanted
to do.'

Watching the British flag rise to the top of the flagpole day after day
convinced Byrne this was what he wanted to do next, even though it
was more than a decade since he last rode a bike, and even then it was
only to mess about on. First, though, he had to learn to walk.

After Selly Oak, he was transferred to Headley Court, where his
injury was put into a different context. 'When I stood on that bomb
it wasn't in my plans,' he says, 'but I accepted it straight away. It is the
cards I have been dealt.'

The bomb was so big it could easily have killed Byrne and the other
men out on foot patrol that day. He knew he'd been lucky, a belief
reinforced by his stay at Headley Court: 'I lost my right leg below my
knee which, if you go to Headley Court, is a scratch. That is the way I
see it.'

A few days after arriving at the Surrey military rehabilitation centre,
he got a call from one of his Army mates telling him that flights to
Australia had been booked and tickets purchased for the final of the
Rugby League World Cup in November.

It normally takes six to eight months for injured soldiers to successfully complete the Headley Court rehabilitation process: Byrne had six weeks. 'In my mind I had to be walking, running again, off the sticks and out of the wheelchair so I could go to Australia and be as normal as possible,' he says.

And so, six weeks later, he left Headley Court with about enough time to pack his bags for Australia. 'I could walk, run and hop on my right leg. I could do everything, so they discharged me completely,' he says. He took his crutches to Australia as back-up, but when a friend dropped a boulder on his foot and broke it, Byrne handed the crutches over to him. 'I was on my own then, but it was the best way to get on with my new leg,' he says.

Before leaving for Australia, he had been told of a Talent Identification Day (ID) at the Mile End Sports Centre in London, organised by ParalympicsGB, where disabled athletes from all over the country have the chance to try multiple sports under one roof. Those with talent are invited back to train for the sport and undergo further tests. On offer for all that autumn day were: Wheelchair Basketball, Wheelchair Tennis, Rowing, Swimming, Wheelchair Fencing, Archery, Wheelchair Rugby, Athletics, Judo, Sitting Volleyball, Cycling, Shooting, Skiing, Sailing, Powerlifting and Football.

As a boy, Byrne got to Black Belt level in Taekwondo; in the Army he'd enjoyed boxing and rugby, but on this particular day, he had eyes for one sport only and that was cycling. Having located the relevant area of the sports centre where the cycling tests were taking place, he parked his wheelchair out of sight, put on his artificial leg and walked over to register his interest. 'There must have been 500 people at the ID day, but Cycling was the only sport I wanted to do. I hid my wheelchair because I did not know how much it would affect the coaches if they saw it,' he says.

Not that he need worry: his results were good enough to see him invited back for further testing and the following year, in April 2009, he was offered a place on the prestigious British Cycling Development Programme. In June that same year, with the backing of the Army, Byrne moved to Manchester, where Britain's elite Olympic and Paralympic Cycling team are based. Accommodation was found for him by the Army and he has their full backing to train until 2012 – with one proviso. 'Go and win some medals,' he says they told him, 'and we will support you.'

And that is what Tel Byrne intends to do, aiming for gold in the Team Sprint and the Individual Kilo, which is where riders race for 1000m against the clock from a standing start. 'There is no point in aiming for second place, is there?' he says. 'You have already lost.'

As to the day in the summer of 2008 that changed the course of his life he has absolutely no regrets. 'I loved the Army but I am lucky enough to have the opportunity to go to London in 2012 and I am going to grab it with both hands and do the best I can.'

Chapter Six

Behind the Scenes

'An athlete cannot run with money in his pockets. He must run with hope in his heart and dreams in his head.'

Emil Zátopek, four-time Olympic gold medallist

There isn't a professional athlete competing on the world stage today who could have started their career without the help of those closest to them, be they parents, coaches or other family members.

Ferrying a talented offspring to the pool in time for a 6am swim session (while the rest of the world slumbers), preparing meals and washing piles of sports kit are the universal roles played by parents and helpers the world over. They are the devoted taxi drivers, cooks and maids who keep the show on the road (at least to begin with).

For some, early promise remains just that and in time, they give up or move on to pursue different interests. Others go on to scale great heights, their parents often continuing to have a major influence. But for some parents, either of children born with a disability or those who have it thrust upon them by circumstance, there are far more basic issues, at least in the early days, to address and navigate, long before their children find an outlet in sport. Whether it is a mother and father who must decide if amputation will help, or hinder, their three-year-old son; a mother driving 100 miles a day for 10 months to be at the bedside of a son struggling with the will to live after a horrific road traffic accident; a father who depends on his wife and family to realise a once-in-a-lifetime dream; or a community coming together to help a young woman rebuild her future after a high-speed riding accident, there is a small army of people behind the scenes who will never have a medal hung around their neck.

***

The first people Jody Cundy thanked after winning Paralympic gold were his parents, Ann, a receptionist, and Alan, a fitter and welder. And, in an illustrious career spanning two sports, Swimming and Cycling, four Games, and five gold medals so far, he's had plenty of practice. From his first success, in Atlanta 1996, to the most recent triumphs on the boards of the Velodrome at Beijing 2008 he knows he owes them a lot. And, since they've been present at all the Games he's attended, he hasn't had to walk that far to thank them. It's not just the obvious support they provided, like driving Jody to training and competitions until he was old enough to get there himself, but because of a decision which fundamentally improved his quality of life.

Born in Wisbech, East Anglia, with a deformed right foot, Jody was fitted with specially adapted boots but by the age of three, his right leg was growing more slowly than the left one. So, on the advice of the surgeon, Ann and Alan decided to amputate Jody's right foot in order to create a stump he could bear his weight on. Once a new artificial leg was attached, he had the freedom to career about like any other youngster and never looked back.

Although amputation had the most obvious impact on Jody's life, there were other significant decisions his parents made. Two years after the amputation, during a school swimming session, he was given an inflatable swimming aid to help with buoyancy but no one realised his incomplete right leg unbalanced his body causing him to roll over, sink and almost drown. Fortunately, a quick-witted parent dived in fully clothed to rescue him.

After that his parents enrolled him in swimming lessons at King's Lynn Swimming Club so he would never be in danger again. Little did they realise they had, unwittingly, literally plunged him into a sport he would later excel at. At first, Jody progressed like any other swimmer, from widths to lengths, before becoming proficient enough to be selected to swim for the club in weekly galas.

By the age of 10 he was regularly racing against non-disabled competition and winning half of all the events entered. Apart from the routine of training and galas there were, periodically, camps to attend which Alan would also take Jody to. Since these were the days before the introduction of Lottery funding, the Cundys met whatever costs were incurred. 'There were very few places where you could get any money,' he recalls. 'I am glad it was a cheap sport.'

In 1994, at the age of 16, Jody got his first big breakthrough when he was selected to represent Britain at the World Championships in Malta. Although he arrived in the Southern European country as a total unknown, within the space of a few hours he was World Champion for the 100m Butterfly, in the S10 category. (In Swimming classes 1–10 are for those with a physical disability, 11–13 for those with a visual impairment and 14 is for athletes with a learning disability).

Chapter Six

Selection for Atlanta in 1996 seemed inevitable, but just in case there was any doubt, Jody broke the world record at the qualifying trials, all of which meant, a few months later and still just 17, he walked into the Olympic Stadium in Atlanta for the Opening Ceremony only to be met by a overwhelming wall of noise. Even as a teenager he knew this was something special. Jody loved his first Paralympic Games and the gold medal he won in the 100m Butterfly.

Jody dived into two more pools in his Paralympic career. First, there was Sydney 2000, where the Australians' love of sport, excellent facilities and enthusiastic crowds contributed to a Games beyond all expectation in terms of athlete experience and, for Jody in particular, success. It was here he took two more golds. And then at Athens 2004 where, despite having his pre-race build-up hampered by glandular fever, he won bronze.

Had Jody retired then his parents would, undoubtedly, have supported him. Instead he continued swimming while also signing up for a Disability Open Day at Newport track where he enjoyed cycling so much he kept going back for more. It wasn't long before his talent was spotted by one of the coaches. Jody entered the National Championships and broke the British record for riders with a disability. A move from one Paralympic sport to another seemed inevitable.

In Olympic sport switching mid-career is rare, although many will recall that Rebecca Romero, who won a silver at Athens 2004 in Rowing, changed to Cycling at Beijing 2008, where she went one better and won gold. In Paralympic sport, it is more common for athletes to change sports and, by 2006, the change was complete for Cundy. Swimming's loss was Cycling's gain. Two years later, in Beijing 2008, his gold medal haul grew from three to five as the Individual Kilo and Team Sprint were added to his growing tally.

Today, Jody Cundy is the fastest man in the world in the Kilo, the distance he specialises in, and one of the most successful riders on the British Cycling squad. Funded by UK Sport, he no longer relies on parental support, although their influence has been ever-present, not least because they instilled in him long ago a belief that hard work yields results. In London there's every chance more gold will be added to the Jody Cundy portfolio. If so, no prizes for guessing who he'll be thanking first.

***

Unlike Jody Cundy, who relied heavily on parental support throughout the early days of his career, Tim Reddish was married with two small children of his own when his Paralympic opportunity came along. Pursuing and fulfilling his dream would not have been possible without their help and cooperation.

Not that his dream took form until later in life. Reddish, who has been chairman of the British Paralympic Association since 2008, didn't run around the streets of Nottingham thinking that one day he would go to the Paralympic Games. That's because he grew up sighted.

Born in 1957 and raised in one of the city's tougher neighbourhoods, he was the eldest of five. With two younger brothers and sisters, the age span between him and his youngest sibling was 13 years. His father, who was an ex-Serviceman, drove buses and lorries; his mum worked behind a bar.

School was a struggle. 'I wasn't the brightest,' Tim now says, and he didn't enjoy the application required to do his homework. Instead he was in and out of trouble, known for making mischief and being cheeky. At 16, he left school and took up an apprenticeship offered through a local supermarket to become a butcher.

Despite growing up with more familial responsibility than most and constantly getting himself in and out of childhood scrapes, sport was always a release, a way of letting off steam and energy. Tim did anything the school offered, including athletics and swimming, as well as playing football on the streets around their home.

And it was through playing football, three months short of his 17th birthday, that he met Val, his future wife. Val's brother, who played on the same football team, set them up on a date at the Football Club Presentation Dance. They were married by the age of 21.

By now, though, Tim was having increasing trouble with his sight, bumping into things and not seeing objects close to him, like doors, which he would walk into. After a spell as a swimming coach Tim, who by then had two young sons to look after, became a leisure facility manager for Nottingham City Council.

And then, he got the worst news ever when he was told he had a genetic eye condition called Retinitis pigmentosa. This condition meant that eventually he would completely lose his sight. It was 1988; Tim was only 31.

To keep fit, he had been swimming at the club, Nottingham Northern Swimming Club, which was based at the same leisure facility he managed. One of the swimmers who regularly trained there was Olympian Maggie Kelly-Hohmann. A breaststroke specialist, Maggie had been to the Montreal 1976 Olympic Games and then to Moscow in 1980, where she won a silver medal in the 4 x 100m Medley Relay. Sometimes Reddish would open the pool early so that she could get some extra time in the run-up to the Seoul 1988 Games, which would be her third, and final, Games.

And then, as Tim's sight continued to deteriorate, came a gesture from one retiring athlete to another aspiring one that would stay with him forever. When Kelly-Hohmann returned from Seoul, she gave Reddish her bronze participation medal, awarded to more than 9,000 athletes and delegates in recognition of attending the Games. 'I want you to go to the Barcelona Paralympic Games in 1992,' she told him, 'and give me your participation medal.'

Today, Paralympic sport is on the nation's conscience. If a youngster with a disability wants to try swimming or tennis they could, in all probability, ring a local club and ask to come along and have a go. In late-1988, it was a different story. 'I had heard about the Paralympic Games, but not to the degree it is on the radar now,' Reddish says. With Kelly-Hohmann's challenge uppermost in his mind, he needed to make some changes. 'I felt I might be a bit old,' he admits, 'so I did some research. I felt if I really committed myself, I could maybe make the team.'

In December 1988, at a coaching session for blind athletes, he met Chris Holmes, the swimmer who won six gold medals at Barcelona in 1992 and is today Director of Paralympic Integration at the London Organising Committee of the Olympic and Paralympic Games (LOCOG). Although Holmes was considerably younger, both shared a 'no compromise' approach to training and instantly got along. 'No compromise meant whatever you did and whatever you wanted in life, swimming was our priority,' says Tim. 'You never miss a training session because you don't feel like it.'

At the same event he talked to Terry Davies, father and coach to child swimming star Sharron Davies, who won a silver medal at Moscow 1980. Tim asked Terry to look at his training log to see what he needed to do to be fast enough to qualify for the British squad. 'Terry agreed – he felt there was a good chance I could make it,' Reddish says.

But he could never have contemplated making the 1992 team had it not been for one person, central and consistent to his story: Val. He knew, if he wanted to go and have a chance of winning a medal he needed to commit to 20 hours a week while simultaneously holding down a job and raising two children. It would mean early mornings and late evenings, and missing out on school events such as parents' evenings, which Val would have to attend alone instead. But the prize at the end of it all was beyond measure. It was Tim's chance to achieve something where it didn't matter if he was visually impaired or not and Val was totally supportive of her husband's goal.

With her support, a club to train at and a programme in place, Tim Reddish began his journey to Barcelona juggling a young family, training and a full-time job. Initially, he continued to do his day job with Nottingham City Council. 'I would work in the day and Val would work at night. If we crossed over, then our parents would babysit. If you want it badly enough, you make it happen,' he says.

In 1992, Reddish achieved what he had worked so hard for – he was selected for the Great Britain team and returned from Barcelona with a silver medal in the 100m Butterfly and a bronze in the 100m Freestyle.

Val and the boys had been there to see it all. But he wanted gold, not silver, next time around in Atlanta and so on his return began to refine the training process he'd started three years earlier.

As was so often the case with athletes from the earlier Paralympic Games, raising funds was often an issue because, in those days, there was still no formal funding in place. Even so, money did amazingly appear and often from the most surprising sources. Reddish and another swimmer, Mark Woods, wanted to go to Singapore to train in the build-up to the Atlanta 1996 Games. Val went into a local travel agent to see if they could help find the cheapest flight tickets possible, explaining why they were needed. Some weeks later, the travel agent called. 'I have got you some tickets,' she said, 'and I have got one for free.' She did this because she wanted to and sought nothing in return. Then, when they got to Singapore, another friend found them a place to stay, while the local Disability Centre welcomed the pair and let them train for free.

There were other acts of kindness and support, too. A local ambulance centre raised enough money to ensure Val could make the journey to Atlanta to support Tim and a disco was held to raise enough funds for the children to go along as well. 'The estate might not have been the best, but the community spirit was fantastic,' Tim says. 'People wanted to help for the right reasons – it wasn't ever patronising.'

Although he first learnt of his eye condition in 1988, it was another seven years, in 1995, before he lost his sight completely. 'When I was diagnosed, I just thought I was short-sighted and clumsy,' he explains. In fact, he had tunnel vision, which together with night blindness, are the main symptoms of retinitis pigmentosa. In the intervening years, the tunnel grew narrower and narrower until eventually he couldn't see anything at all.

As the Atlanta Games approached there was another decision to be faced, as Tim and Val still needed to raise more money if they were all to go. In the end they sold their much-loved VW Camper Van for £450 to make the very last payment. Did they regret it? Not for one moment. Tim wanted to compete at the highest level and together they made choices to give him the best chance of achieving this. One year those choices included taking the whole family to Butlins Holiday Park in Minehead, Somerset, where, as it happened, a top swimming club was training at the same time. As they were both working towards a common competitive goal, Reddish asked if he could join them as they trained, but the coach said no. 'I don't think you would be able to fit in,' Tim recalls being told.

Another reason he had wanted to swim with the club was because they trained from 6am until 7.30am, which would mean he could train while the family slept so they didn't miss holiday time together. After being turned down, Val took Tim to the pool for 7.30am and he trained, alone, once the club had left.

So for a week, other swimmers, and probably visitors, stared at the man with the white cane as he made his way to the water, but once in it no one would have known he was visually impaired. To the uninitiated he swam no differently to anyone else as he used a method of counting each stroke to make sure he knew where he was and when he needed to make a turn.

In the end, though, Reddish's perseverance, determination and unquestionable swimming skills made a formidable impression. By the end of the week the coach approached him and apologised but by then, he had simply got on with it.

The attitude of the coach at the holiday park could not have been in starker contrast to the welcome he was given by coach Bill Furness when he asked if he could transfer from his local club to Nova Centurion Swimming Club, where Furness coached. This was a far bigger club with more experience and pool time on offer. 'He was one of the best coaches in the country,' Reddish explains. And if he wanted to be the best, he needed to surround himself with like-minded individuals.

Years later, Bill Furness achieved recognition of his own. Today he coaches Rebecca Adlington, the swimmer no one had heard of before Beijing, who went on to win two gold medals and break the longest-standing world record in swimming, the women's 800m Freestyle.

'We were honest with each other,' says Reddish. 'We decided to give it a go and see if, between us, we could make it work.' In fact, he says, Bill Furness saw him as an asset to his squad because of the example he set. 'I never missed a work out,' he recalls.

Perhaps today's elite athletes could learn something from the attitude of Tim Reddish, Chris Holmes and other athletes of that era. 'It isn't about kudos for us,' Tim says. 'We went out and made things happen in a positive way.' And they did so without a big fanfare and usually on a shoestring budget.

Reddish lived out his dream and went on to compete at two more Paralympic Games: at Atlanta 1996, where he won silver in the 200m Individual Medley and bronze in the 100m Freestyle, and at Sydney 2000, where he won another silver in the 4 x 100m Medley Relay before retiring with five Paralympic medals from three Games.

His dream, and ultimate successes, had a huge impact on him and his family. 'It gave me a second chance at life,' he admits. But none of the medals or accolades he went on to achieve would have been possible without the total support of those closest to him and years of hard work on his part. 'I didn't make sacrifices, because I could have stopped at any time, ' he says, 'but Val and the boys did.'

That said, no one in the Reddish family regrets the journey, or the experiences, for one minute. 'We would do the same again,' Tim continues. 'The boys gained from it in life, as well as me: they loved being around the athletes and visiting places around the world.'

There may have been sacrifices, but they all shared in the journey. And they weren't the only ones to benefit. In 1992, Maggie Kelly-Hohmann, the Olympic swimmer who first challenged Tim to compete at the Paralympic Games, received a present – Tim Reddish's participation medal from the Barcelona Paralympic Games.

***

No parent expects to wake up one Saturday morning looking forward to a family weekend ahead only to discover, by the end of it, one of their children will never walk again. But when an event of such personal magnitude does happen, sometimes help appears from the most unlikely places. And it continues to come for years after the initial event, or so seemed to be the case with Clare Strange.

Maybe it was the kind of friends she attracted growing up in the small Buckinghamshire village of Radnage, or perhaps it was because it was the type of place where no one needed guidance on how to look out for each other. Whatever it was, a theme running through Strange's story is the readiness with which a large circle of friends, from all the different areas of her life, offered and delivered help when it was most needed.

Although Clare played any sport on offer as a child what she loved most was competing in mounted games on her horse, Dudley. By the age of 13 she wanted to win the Horse of the Year Show as that was the ultimate competition – and where mounted games as a branch of equestrian sport first began.

Fun and fast-moving, mounted games is an exhilarating sport, which involves riders and their ponies competing in a variety of obstacle- and relay-type races. Excellent riding skills and good hand-to-eye coordination are essential. The concept was originally inspired by Prince Philip, who asked the then director of the Horse of the Year Show, Colonel Sir Mike Ansell, if he could come up with a mounted competition so that ordinary children could enjoy the thrill and excitement of competing without necessarily having to own their own expensive pony.

In 1957, the inaugural Mounted Games Championships took place at the Horse of the Year Show competing for the Prince Philip Cup. It was a huge success but as Pony Club rules state riders can only compete until the age of 14, there was no progression for older riders. This led to the founding in 1984 of the Mounted Games Association of Great Britain, which enabled riders over the age of 14 to compete. There are three categories: Minis (under 12), Junior (under 17) and Open, for any age, and today, more than 25 years later, mounted games are enjoyed throughout the world.

It was in this 'mad and crazy' world Clare excelled, enjoying jumping off Dudley as he was galloping along and then, having retrieved the relevant item, leaping back on. And she was good, representing the south of England at competitive level and in all likelihood, going on to ride for England one day.

It was usual for Clare to spend weekends competing and so it was something of a rarity for her to find that 10 days after her 18th birthday, she had an unexpected weekend off. It seemed the perfect time to host a belated birthday party for the extended family. With no pressure to get ready for competition, she decided to spend the morning with her younger brother Dan and friend Richard, taking the horses for some gentle morning exercise through the woods close to where they lived.

There were trees all around and so as the three galloped along, they were careful to weave a path around the trunks. And then suddenly there was a tree trunk right in Clare and Dudley's way. An instant decision was needed, so Clare leaned her body over to the left so that she wouldn't be too close to the tree but her sudden shift in weight threw his balance and Dudley went right instead. Clare took a glancing blow to the side of her head from the tree, forcing her off Dudley. The impact caused the top half of her body to instantly stop but the bottom half carried on through, dislocating Clare's spine and severing her spinal cord.

Dan immediately dismounted and rushed to his sister's aid. As he did so, the two saddled horses continued through the woods. When they galloped past the nearby farm, friends realised something terrible had happened and rushed to help. After the alarm was raised it set in motion a train of coincidences and acts of kindness which undoubtedly aided Clare's recovery.

As it was clear a suspected spinal injury had occurred, and not wanting to risk further damage by transferring Clare by road, an air ambulance was dispatched. Although Clare has no memory of the accident site, even though she was fully conscious throughout, she remembers vividly being loaded into the helicopter. She knew the pilot and he told her a joke, which, perhaps surprisingly given the circumstances, made her laugh. Instead of heading home to prepare for her 18th birthday and a houseful of guests, Clare was on her way to Stoke Mandeville. By the time she did go home, some months later, both the house and her life had changed beyond measure.

Within hours of being admitted, she asked the doctor the question she suspected she could really answer for herself: 'So, is this permanent then?' 'He told me I had done a really good job in dislocating my spine at T9. You normally only ever sever a spinal cord if you are shot or stabbed,' she explains. So, yes, it was permanent. Impossible as it is to imagine how anyone could absorb this kind of news and adjust to a whole new way of life, let alone a sporty, competitive teenager, one more coincidence took place that eased the transition, at least in the early days.

Clare was then in her last year at school, studying for A-levels, and her attention had been focused on what she might do next. Training to become a physiotherapist had appealed for some time. Remarkably, six weeks earlier, she had done work experience at the very spinal unit where she was now being treated as a patient, which meant there were physiotherapists, staff and even patients she knew from recent visits.

Chapter Six

Whether it was the familiar faces, the constant stream of visitors from horse riding, hockey or school, or the support of the unit's staff, who only ever concentrated on what could be achieved in the future, rather than what could not, she was on the road to recovery.

For Clare it was all about getting out of hospital and back home as soon as possible. She also realised very early on that it could have been a lot worse, probably because when she first arrived and was recovering in the high dependency unit, the first patient she was aware of had broken his neck so high up he was on a ventilator. It put it all into perspective.

As the days passed and she grew stronger, visitors arrived in their droves armed with helpful information and offering what support they could, another example of the willingness of those also affected by news of the accident to help. Clare's horse-riding coach researched the different types of sports' wheelchairs available and how to get involved in wheelchair hockey. Whatever other sports she might try in the future, she knew returning to the hard-and-fast world of mounted games was out of the question. After the thrill of jumping off a galloping horse and then jumping back on it, being able to sit on it alone would now require the help of others and was never going to cut it.

In hospital her affinity with sport found a welcome outlet as taking part in daily physical activity is core to the rehabilitation of spinal injuries. They might not have been the sports Clare would have experienced before, or the ones she would later take part in, but they were interesting ways to do rehabilitation exercises. And they all worked different, essential areas, so table tennis helped with balance while archery improved strength. For the patient, rehab is also a full-time occupation as it takes place from 9am to 5pm. Soon her timetable was so full, friends could no longer visit when they felt like it: they had to ring up and check first. All of which meant that, four months after being airlifted to Stoke Mandeville, Clare was ready to go home – although it was rather different to the home she remembers leaving on the morning of 27 September 1997.

By a stroke of luck, her parents already lived in a bungalow, which meant few adjustments were needed in terms of accessibility but other modifications had to be made. Unknown to Clare, a group of friends had arrived to help out. A new door to her bedroom appeared, fresh from the James Bond set where a friend was working as a carpenter. Others set about transforming the room into an en suite and creating another bathroom for Clare's parents and two siblings to use.

'It was a bit like [the television programme] DIY SOS,' Clare recalls, 'that is how it is in a village like that, everyone mucks in. On the day of my accident one family turned up to pick up one dog while another family picked up the other dog. People just do that – they step up.' But that wasn't all. By now in need of a wheelchair and an adapted car, friends from school and the horse-riding and hockey communities embarked on an extensive fund-raising campaign, which eventually raised a breathtaking £30,000 to help Clare with some of the basics required in her new life.

While friends provided support and funds, Clare set about picking up her life where it left off, although this wasn't without its challenges. Home from hospital in February in 1998, she returned to school with the idea that she would still complete her A-levels that summer despite a four-month absence. The plan didn't work, however, and she ended up repeating her final school year, something she really didn't enjoy. 'It was horrible,' she says. 'All your friends are going to university, beginning work or travelling – they are doing something different. It is that key shift in life and yet for me, this chaos had happened in my life and I had to go back to school for another year.'

Although not an easy decision, she knew that if she didn't get her qualifications at that point she would always regret it. Besides, by spring 1998, something else had come into Clare's life that required extra focus.

During her months at Stoke Mandeville a few wheelchair basketball sessions for patients had been held. Although not particularly strong then, she immediately enjoyed being involved in a physically demanding sport. But there's a big difference between trying a sport and becoming proficient at it, and Clare knew it.

She joined her local club, Milton Keynes Aces, and went along for the first day of training. Just three girls turned up to have a try but Clare was the only one to go back: she had glimpsed something she wanted to be a part of. Once again she called upon the resources available to her and as well as club training, she would drag her friends into the sports hall during school lunch hours and have them help with basic skills. Since neither her shooting or passing was very good at that stage, she relied on her best friend, Jo Rush, to patiently join her on court, returning the ball to her day after day until she got better.

It all paid off, though. In April 1998, just two months after leaving hospital and only six months since her accident, Clare Strange was invited to attend a Women's Development Day in Chester, the aim of which was to introduce more women to the sport.

At club level, wheelchair basketball is a mixed event, but at Paralympic level, the sport is single-sex, so the more women who took up the sport, the stronger the British team would be. Despite the fact she, 'didn't know the rules, couldn't move my chair and was shockingly terrible', those watching Clare clearly saw something. She was invited to return the next day and take part in a Great Britain squad day.

For the 18-year-old teenager who had seen her life turned on its head in the preceding six months this was a surreal moment. Thanks in no small part to the unswerving support of her family and friends together with her own determination, hard work and vision for the future, the door to a new world of competitive sport was very much ajar and ready to step through.

***

That door is now much more likely to stay open for athletes like Clare Strange than in the past. In 1997, the year she broke her back, the World Class Performance Programme was introduced and radically changed the way British athletes were funded. No longer so dependent on informal support networks such as family and friends, the introduction of the National Lottery in 1994 meant that the nation's brightest sporting talent could now access greater amounts of cash from a formal, structured source. When Lottery funding was just starting up, the money went to the athletes most likely to succeed and that is still the abiding principle.

Today, a transparent and effective funding strategy is in place for all Olympic and Paralympic sports. The exceptions to this are non-disabled

Football, Paralympic 5-a-side and 7-a-side Football, and Wheelchair Tennis, which UK Sport do not fund as the sports are deemed 'able to self fund'. As a result, at Beijing 2008 Britain's Paralympic team was better funded than any that had gone before.

Between Athens 2004 and Beijing 2008, nearly £30 million was invested across multiple Paralympic sports to achieve excellence at elite level. That sum has risen to an investment of nearly £48 million in the current London 2012 cycle.

Money is awarded to both Olympic and Paralympic athletes in one of two ways. First, UK Sport, the body responsible for investing in high-performance sport in Britain, provides each sport's governing body with funds to enable the sport to be competitive in the world's sporting arenas. It is the job of the performance director of each sport to use the cash to create structures and methods which result in elite success. These include employing world-class sports coaches, developing sports science, providing appropriate training facilities, creating athlete development plans and putting in place lifestyle programmes to provide athletes with everything they need to create a winning environment.

Typically, this support is worth around £55,000 per athlete, per year, for Podium athletes – those most likely to come back with medals from the next Games – and £30,000 per athlete, per year, for Development athletes – those who are on their way up. When making funding awards, UK Sport looks at both past performance and future potential of athletes within a sport to deliver medals, as well as the number of medals available at an Olympic and Paralympic Games. Swimming, for example, had a massive 140 gold medals on offer at the Beijing 2008 Paralympic Games whereas there were just four in Rowing.

In general, sports that have yielded the most success at Olympic and Paralympic level receive bigger budgets, running into tens of millions of pounds. So, for example, between 2009 and 2013, Rowing received £27 million, Cycling £26 million, Athletics £25 million and Swimming £25 million, making them the four best-funded sports.

Money can also be awarded directly to an athlete through an Athlete Personal Award (APA). Designed to contribute to an athlete's costs in competing at elite level, the APA varies. On average, a Podium athlete receives approximately £19,500 a year, while a Development athlete receives £5,300.

As the APA is only a contribution to costs athletes can earn additional income from other sources, including salaries, sponsorships and prize money, up to a maximum of £64,200 a year. Once an athlete's earnings exceed this amount the APA is reduced, pound for pound, by any excess amount. Athletes who earn far in excess of their APA are 'means-tested out'. Although there is a perception that elite athletes can name their price when it comes to commercial deals, out of about 1,200 athletes funded by UK Sport, in 2011 fewer than 15 Olympic athletes and three Paralympic athletes were 'means-tested out'.

Long before September 1979, when Clare Strange was born, athletes who competed for Britain at Paralympic level funded their own involvement or relied on being bankrolled, almost always by parents and friends. Caz Walton, who attended her first Paralympic Games at Tokyo 1964, remembers her parents paying for everything. 'There was no finance at all,' she said. It was the same for earlier athletes, including Margaret Maughan who won Britain's first Paralympic gold medal in Archery at Rome 1960, and for those who followed her. Many had jobs and careers, fitting these responsibilities around training and racing commitments.

***

Clare Strange grew up loving sport – it made her world tick. If she wasn't dreaming of riding Dudley at the best equestrian event available to her, she was thinking of playing hockey for Britain. Breaking her back didn't change that. And, in fact, one key factor aiding her recovery after the accident was the number of different sports she encountered during her time at Stoke Mandeville. So when the selectors asked her to attend her first Great Britain squad training day just six months after the accident, this only re-ignited a familiar flame. 'I always wanted to compete at the highest level and this was another opportunity to do that,' she says.

At the end of her first day's training in Chester the coach had told everyone who attended they had a chance of going to the Wheelchair Basketball World Championships later in the year. Clare was so astonished by the suggestion she thought it must be a joke but with the very real possibility of making the squad on the horizon, she went home and considered how to put around her a support team that would help reach that goal.

The most important area she needed expert help with was basic fitness and strength so she found a local instructor to assist with that while continuing to rely on non-disabled friends to develop on-court skills. Training hard and using the expertise and goodwill of others turned out to be the perfect decision as in October 1998, just a year and a month after her accident, Clare Strange was named in the British Wheelchair Basketball Squad for the World Championships and was on her way to Australia to compete.

Soon after that the carrot of competing at the Sydney 2000 Games was dangled tantalisingly close. 'I remember someone saying maybe you could make Sydney and me saying there will be another Paralympic Games after that and maybe I will be good enough in 2004,' Clare says. But she was more than good enough for the 12-strong Sydney squad and in October 2000, she arrived in Australia to find a country – and a city – that fully embraced all the Paralympic Movement had to offer. 'They love sport. The Olympic Games had finished and they just wanted more of it,' she explains.

The Games were superbly organised and enthusiastically received and enhanced by the thousands of volunteers who make a Games possible. There were also more than a million spectators, nearly treble the number who had attended the Atlanta Games.

Strange had never been to a Paralympic Games before and so she had no idea what it would be like. 'The place was packed every day,' she recalls. 'I hadn't expected that. This is the Paralympic Games, not the Olympic Games – I was surprised. You could not get around without being stopped.'

The skill, speed and excitement of Wheelchair Basketball means that it's consistently one of the most popular spectator sports on the Paralympic programme. It's also one of the oldest, having been played in the first Paralympic Games in Rome, 1960. Played between two teams of five, the aim is to score in the opponent's basket and prevent the other team from scoring. It's fast and fun to watch and employs similar rules to Basketball, including the same size court and basket height. The scoring system is also the same: one point for a free-throw, two for a normal field basket and three points if the successful shot is taken from behind the arc of the three-point line. Unlike Basketball, though, wheelchair players can, and do, fall out of their chairs, which adds to the tension and on-court drama.

Players pass and dribble the ball and must release it to another player or bounce it after every two pushes of the wheels. All players are given a point value depending on their level of disability. Wheelchair Basketball has both male and female teams and is played by two teams of five players each. Depending on their functional abilities a point value from 0.5 (most severely disabled) to 4.5 is given to each player. Five players out of 12 from each team are on the court during playtime and throughout the game the total point value of each team must not exceed 14 points.

Although British athletes have been prolific medal winners in other Paralympic sports, Britain has yet to excel on the world stage in the women's game. At the Sydney 2000 Games the team finished eighth, well outside the medals. The team again finished eighth at Athens 2004 and repeated that performance at Beijing 2008, and is now ranked sixth in the world.

As UK Sport's funding is based on past results as well as future potential, the women's team is on 'basic funding' whereas the men's team is fully funded in recognition of its medal pedigree, winning silver at Atlanta 1996 and picking up bronze at Athens 2004 and Beijing 2008. Wheelchair Basketball receives a funding award of nearly £4.5m for the 2009–13 cycle to cover both the men's and women's teams.

This is the third-highest award, behind Disability Swimming (almost £9.9m) and Athletics (£6.5m).

Today Clare Strange is one of the leaders of the women's Wheelchair Basketball team but if you think it's a glamorous life of public appearances and sponsorship endorsements, you'd be wrong. She first received funding of £4,000 in 2009, increased to £6,000 in 2010, and that means like many athletes who have gone before, she must work to supplement her income and fit training around other commitments.

Despite the early-morning and late-night training sessions, the requirement to work and the need to attend events to fund-raise, representing Britain for over a decade and the Championships she attended are not experiences she would ever have missed.

Like so many Paralympic athletes catapulted into an unplanned new life, her journey from the devastating riding accident, which required emergency hospital admission, to elite athlete competing at the biggest multi-sports event in the world involved the help, support and commitment of numerous supporters who will never get to wear a Great Britain tracksuit, take part in a spectacular, joyful Olympic and Paralympic parade through the streets of London or meet royalty and premiers. But, as Clare's story shows, they are all-too often willing to play their part.

**

You don't have to scratch deep among the Paralympic community to find examples of team members, past or present, who came to competitive disability sport because of an accident. Whether it's the story of Margaret Maughan, Britain's first gold medallist, or Tom Aggar, one of the most recent participants, there are many similar stories.

When tragedy strikes, medical attention is first directed towards the injured individual to establish survival and then, when the immediate danger has passed, towards the long road to transition and psychological acceptance. But for the parents, who must adjust to a whole new set of circumstances as suddenly as their injured child while still continuing to act as mothers and fathers, it's very often agonising and heartbreaking to watch. In time, a newly paralysed patient is put to work learning fresh skills to regain independence but at first, in the early days, parents can do little but wait and hope. One such parent who went through it all was Cynthia Norfolk, whose son, Peter, had a teenage motorbike crash.

As a child he liked nothing more than kicking a football around. The youngest of three children, with an older brother and sister, Peter started school life near Twickenham rugby ground before moving on to boarding school in Southampton at the age of 12. He participated in everything on offer, from diving to squash, and excelled at most, although somewhat surprisingly given that years later it would be the sport in which he dominated the wheelchair world, not at tennis.

Having spent more time playing sport than studying, Peter left school to work in the hotel and catering trade, initially as a trainee waiter at the prestigious Hyde Park Hotel (now called the Mandarin Oriental Hotel) in London's exclusive Knightsbridge. Peter loved his job and the environment, but he was commuting from his parents' home in Surrey to the hotel on his bike and the days, already long, were made harder by the journey. That year, 1979, was also a long, cold winter and he kept falling off his bike. In the end he decided it made more sense to take a job closer to home as an assistant manager in a restaurant.

With time off at Christmas Peter decided to make the most of the break from work and his new three-week-old motorbike, and head over to see his girlfriend on Boxing Day. As he rode through the pretty Surrey country lanes, quiet thanks to the holiday period, he didn't even see the raised manhole cover in the road. He hit it full-on, catapulting forward over the handlebars and into the road. The bike carried on moving and struck him in the back.

The bike had barely a scratch on it. Peter, on the other hand, was seriously injured with a broken back at T4/5 and a broken shoulder blade, collarbone, sternum and two ribs.

Appalling as his injuries were, they could have been worse. A woman who lived close to the road thought she heard something and came out to investigate, as did her boyfriend, who happened to be an off-duty ambulance driver. This meant back-up arrived almost immediately. Nevertheless, 19-year-old Peter Norfolk was in a pretty bad way and after a few days in a local hospital, he was transferred to Stoke Mandeville.

Even there, surrounded by specialist equipment and knowledge, there were problems and setbacks. On more than one occasion, Peter stopped breathing. In the midst of it all, however, one person was there throughout: Cynthia Norfolk, Peter's mum, who gave up her job to make the 100-mile round trip from their Surrey home every day to be at her son's side. The accident, though, was much harder for his father to handle: after the Christmas break was over he had to go back to work. 'In those days, you had no choice – you did not take a day off,' he says.

So, while Peter's father came at weekends, his mother visited him every day. 'There was a stage when I wasn't going to last and she was holding my hand. It was as well she was there, for sure,' says Peter. 'There are times when you lie there and think, what is the point? You are in all this pain and have all these things wrong with you. That's when you need your support. You don't need them to say much, you just need them to be there.'

Whatever inner anguish Cynthia Norfolk was going through, including the shattered dreams for her son's future she was wrestling with, she never showed it. Instead she did what she instinctively did best: she sat with her son through 10 months of pain, anger and adjustment, and being told the news – two months into his hospital stay – that he would never walk again. Without doubt her support, more than anything, is what pulled him through.

By the end of 1980, Peter was home from hospital and sleeping in the study of his parents' house as they all got used to the change. And then, within two months, he was offered his own bungalow and moved out.

After that he went back to work at the same local hotel he had been employed at before the accident. Angry and frustrated by what life had thrown at him, as well as the restrictions of a new life in a wheelchair, he found the distraction of being at work really helped. 'In those days there was a lot of discrimination,' he says, 'but working was fun and new and I was different. I always wanted to go back because I wanted to do something with my life irrespective of being in a chair.'

He also had no illusions about a miracle cure or a return to the life he once led: 'I realised I was never going to walk again.' And that only left him with two choices: 'Either your life stops, or your life stops and starts again. If it starts again, you get off your backside and go and do something." He opted for the latter.

Much as Peter enjoyed working in the hotel trade, the long hours and lack of a career path got him down. In the 1980s, in a very different age of disability awareness (or lack of it) he was never going to achieve what he really wanted, which was to run his own hotel restaurant bar. It just wasn't going to happen, and so he left.

In the summer of 1989, Peter did two very important things in his life. First he went to watch Wheelchair Tennis at the Stoke Mandeville International Games. Quite why anyone watched tennis at all in those days is a mystery since the courts were placed next door to the hospital crematorium. If smoke appeared above the courts, everyone knew the reason why.

Human mortality aside, Peter sat there and watched as two of the then best players in the world competed in front of him. He came to his own conclusion. 'In my own arrogance and pig-headedness I thought, you are not that good,' he said of the players. But then he himself went out on court and found out it was much harder than it looked. It was just the incentive he needed to take up the game: he was nearly 29.

The second thing to happen was that Peter left the hotel industry and decided he wanted to start his own wheelchair dealership so that he could sell chairs to fellow users like himself. In 1989, with an investment of £2,000, Equipment for the Physically Challenged, or EPC, was established in Farnborough, Hampshire. Peter has been mixing elite Wheelchair Tennis with running a business ever since. 'I always tell people there is nothing you can't do. You can't walk, but you can do whatever you want to do. Whatever your dream, is you can do it,' he says.

Whether Peter Norfolk was dreaming about Paralympic glory in 1989 after he'd decided that the best Wheelchair Tennis players in the world really weren't that good, or not, he was never going to beat anyone unless he first learned how to play. When he returned home from Stoke Mandeville, he went to the tennis centre in Aldershot and with characteristic directness, got straight to the point. 'Are you the coach?' he asked a retired army Lt-Colonel on the courts. When the Lt-Colonel confirmed he was, Peter said, 'I want you to teach me to play tennis.'

As it turned out, this was one of the best requests he ever made. 'Being a retired colonel there was no such word as "can't" – it suited my personality,' he explains. So, for two hours every morning, from 8am to 10am, Peter made the commitment to turn up for training, as did the colonel. Afterwards, Peter would then set off on his sales' calls, travelling up to 60,000 miles a year, selling, servicing and maintaining chairs as he built up a fledgling business. In those days he did everything himself, from selling to repairing; today, he has a team to help.

No matter how much work he had to do later in the day, or the state of the weather, come rain or shine, he would always turn up for training and relished the changes he could feel. 'I loved it,' he says. 'The fitter you are, the easier it is. I played four or five times a week for two hours at a time but it was more a case of what I could afford. It wasn't until before Athens, in 2004, I got funding.'

Wheelchair tennis first started in the USA in 1976. Today it is one of the fastest-growing wheelchair sports in the world, with more than 6,000 people now thought to be playing the game in 70 countries right across the globe. The sport was a demonstration event at Seoul 1988 before being accepted onto the Paralympic programme at Barcelona 1992. Quad events were introduced at Athens 2004.

To compete at the Paralympic Games a player must have a permanent mobility-related physical disability that results in substantial loss of function in one or both of the lower extremities. To compete in the Quad division that player must, additionally, have a permanent physical disability which results in substantial loss of function in one or both upper extremities, in three or more limbs.

At London 2012 there will be six medal events: the Men's and Women's Singles, Men's and Women's Doubles, Mixed Quad Singles and Quad Doubles. Although the rules of the game are similar to Tennis there are some key differences. For a start the ball is allowed to bounce twice and while the first bounce must be inside the court, the second is allowed outside the court markings. Matches are the best of three sets.

Peter Norfolk was initially a men's Wheelchair Tennis player rather than a Quad, who narrowly missed out on selection for Atlanta in 1996. But over the years he had been gradually losing power, feeling and control in his right side because of an insidious build-up of fluid on the spinal column. Eventually he had a cordectomy. This is where the spine is cut in half so pressure can be released and fluid drained off. It stabilises, but does not cure the problem. The operation successfully removed the build-up of fluid but also meant Peter would have only about half the power and no finite movements or feeling on his right hand side.

And so the quad division – for those who have three or more limbs affected – was the only option if he wanted to keep playing. It took him four years to learn how to play, let alone win the biggest tournaments in the world. 'I lost my first matches. I had to work my way up, to go to tournaments with targets and to gradually better them,' he says. 'First, my target would be to make the quarter-finals, then the semi-finals and then the final. Once I was in the final, the target was to win.'

After four years and a considered plan of action, Peter Norfolk wheeled onto court at the Olympic Tennis Centre at the Athens 2004 Games to face David Wagner of the USA. He won in straight sets: 6-3, 6-2. The inaugural winner of the Quad Singles title was also Britain's first-ever Paralympic tennis gold medallist. Not bad for someone who didn't even take up Wheelchair Tennis until after the age of 30.

The achievement may have cost around £100,000 in terms of lost business earnings, training and travel costs, the extra staff needed to cover for Norfolk while he was away, and the minute, yet expensive, adjustments to chair components needed at this level. It certainly required mental toughness, first to learn the game and then to dedicate hour upon hour, week after week, year on year, to perfect the skills needed to play – and stay – at the highest level. And yet, as was the case with Tim Reddish 20 years earlier, in the run-up to Barcelona 1992, it couldn't have been done without the support of Norfolk's family. 'They are fully behind me,' he says. 'It is a commitment by all of us.'

But for one particular onlooker winning in Athens meant something else. For Cynthia Norfolk, who a quarter of a century earlier, drove thousands of miles for 10 months to keep a bedside watch over her son's progress, it was a moment money can't buy. First she'd been there when it was just about survival, then she'd seen his transition from motorbike casualty to an independent person who went back to work. Now he was winning gold on the biggest sporting stage in the world for athletes with a disability. Victory, for her, in an ancient Greek city on a late September night in 2004 had only one value. Priceless.

Chapter Seven

Pushing the Boundaries

'Courage doesn't always roar. Sometimes courage is the quiet voice at the end of the day saying, "I will try again tomorrow."'

Mary Anne Radmacher, writer and artist

Sometimes there are moments in a sport's development or an athlete's career that catapult unsuspecting individuals into the spotlight and generate a media frenzy. These moments can be magical, or controversial, inspiring or insensitive; what unites them all is that they stay in the memory long after the event that caused them is over. These are the moments that can change awareness and expectation forever.

Recall the graceful, charismatic Jamaican runner Usain Bolt winning over the watching world as he flew down the track at Beijing 2008 to take the 100m crown in a new world record of 9.69 seconds. When he lined up for the 200m, a second gold medal was delivered. And then a third in the 4 x 100m Relay.

The Paralympic Games has its own heroes, but those who have the greatest impact are the ones who achieve such dominance in a particular sport: they set new benchmarks others can only aspire to and the public sits up and takes note. These defining moments, somehow, change our perception and admiration. And then, just occasionally the feats of these athletes transcend the sporting arena and cross over into society.

Tanni Grey-Thompson has had plenty of defining moments of her own in her career to choose from. Was it the time she won her first Paralympic medal, a bronze, at Seoul 1988 or the four golds that followed at Barcelona 1992? Perhaps the crushing disappointment of losing three of those four titles at Atlanta 1996 and then being told, at the age of 27, it was time to retire? Was it proving everyone wrong with four gold medals at Sydney 2000 or a moment of crass television history that people remember about her most? Or was it the moment her racing career really began with a £2,000 donation from Peter, her father, who gave her the money after graduation so she could spend a year concentrating on racing in Barcelona without the need to look for a job?

As far as the public was concerned it was probably Tanni's regular appearances on the start line of the London Marathon – an event she won six times in total – that first caught their attention. Being associated with, and winning, such a high-profile, global race did her reputation no harm nor did her willingness to share the experience with viewers. One year she even allowed the BBC to strap a 2kg camera to her wheelchair and fit a microphone to provide a better insight into the skill and endurance wheelchair racing demands. Not that these marathons were ever particularly lucrative. According to her autobiography, *Seize the Day*, the most prize money Tanni ever picked up for these victories was less than £1,000.

One big factor in raising her profile though, and that of elite sport for athletes with a disability in general, was the role BBC sports presenter Helen Rollason played. Engaging and knowledgeable, Rollason was a true sports fan who brought passion to her reporting and appreciated and understood Paralympic sport for what it was. She covered the Barcelona 1992 and Atlanta 1996 Games (both for the BBC) and helped to ensure disability sport took its place on mainstream television. In addition to this she was the first female presenter of the BBC's flagship sports programme, *Grandstand*, and perhaps getting to the top in a notoriously tough and male-dominated profession gave her a natural affinity with Grey-Thompson. Whatever it was, the two became friends and Tanni invited Rollason to her wedding to cyclist Ian Thompson in Cardiff in May 1999.

By then, however, Rollason, one of the brightest female television presenters, had been diagnosed with colon cancer, which later spread to her liver and lungs. By the time of the wedding she was too ill to attend and died in August 1999. She was 43.

So it was with some irony that an award presented to Tanni Grey-Thompson in Rollason's memory at the BBC Sports Personality of the Year in 2000 was followed by one of the biggest sporting gaffes in the history of Paralympic Games coverage – the ripples of which are still felt today.

A lack of knowledge about Paralympic sport and what it takes to excel at the highest level still exists. This may be less entrenched and less patronising than it once was, but it certainly hasn't been eradicated. Countless athletes have recounted tales from everyday life about a lack of awareness, no matter how well-meaning or accidental. Take the example given by a wheelchair athlete on a recent shopping trip to a supermarket with her husband. Once the required items had been paid for by said athlete, the cashier gave the change back to the athlete's husband. Or the time another wheelchair athlete approached an automatic door only to find a member of the public insisting on standing in front of the sensor until the athlete had passed through. What the athlete wanted to say, but didn't, was that the door opens for someone in a wheelchair in the same way it opens for an non-disabled person – there is no need to stand and 'hold' it. Sometimes these incidents arise out of a lack of insight, other times it's just a well-meaning, if over-eager, desire to help.

Tanni Grey-Thompson has never thought of, or seen, herself as any different to anyone else. She didn't take up sport to show the world what athletes with a disability could do: she participated because she enjoyed it and then discovered she was exceptionally good at it. That she touched the hearts and minds of those watching on her path from sports devotee to World and Paralympic champion was an entirely unconscious by-product of her talent, commitment and hard work.

And although she probably didn't realise it at the time it was this attitude, together with a number of unforgettable performances and humbling moments, which enshrined her in the nation's hearts. By the time she returned from Sydney 2000, her profile was at an all-time high and once the euphoria of the Games had died down, she too, like everyone else, was looking forward to re-living the year's sporting highlights at the BBC's annual Sports Personality of the Year awards.

These were, after all, the Games where Steve Redgrave kept more than 6.5 million Britons from their beds as they stayed up to watch him win an historic fifth gold medal in five consecutive Games. Along with Matthew Pinsent, Tim Foster and James Cracknell, the British Coxless Four raced the 2000m of Penrith Lakes to hold off the Italian crew by the narrowest of margins, just 0.38 seconds. There seemed little doubt who would be the recipient of the main prize.

But as the ceremony went on, there was another presentation to be made: the Helen Rollason Award in memory of the sports presenter, which is given 'for outstanding achievement in the face of adversity'. The inaugural award in 1999 – the year Rollason died – was made to horse trainer Jenny Pitman, the first woman to train a Grand National winner in 1983, who also overcame thyroid cancer. Since the award's inception there have been 12 recipients. All have been British apart from South African Paralympic sprinter, Oscar Pistorius, in 2007.

Much to Tanni's surprise she realised that the award was being made to her. The assumption was that her disability automatically meant she must always have faced an uphill battle to get to the top, but she felt being singled out for the award missed the point: 'I don't think there has been much adversity. I grew up in a middle-class home with parents who could afford to help me do things. They were educated and helped smooth the path. My parents did not shower me with money but they opened up the way. When they made the announcement, it was about everything I had overcome.'

After all, Tanni hadn't overcome anything different to the hundreds of other athletes gathered there that night. She worked just as hard, obtained a travelling grant from the Winston Churchill Memorial Trust so she could go to Australia to train with one of the best wheelchair coaches in the business and followed a training programme that required commitment, perseverance and a lot of hard work. And when it came to race day she executed her plans with precision and vision.

Tanni trained 15 times a week, every week, and had two weeks off a year, in October. She trained on Christmas and Boxing Day, and missed plenty of birthdays and family gatherings in pursuit of excellence. In

1996, she went out and got a job that would help her develop and refine the skills needed to support her once her competitive days were over. And she was happy with it all. Of course there were challenges along the way, but they were different to 'overcoming' her disability.

As far as she was concerned, she was simply an elite athlete at the top of her game who had travelled the world and enjoyed experiences few others, non-disabled or not, will ever know. It is one of the great privileges of being exceptionally good at sport. She'd competed on the biggest sporting stages in the world – including demonstration races at the Olympic Games – met politicians and royalty, and been decorated for her achievements. Adversity is not a word that features in the Tanni Grey-Thompson vocabulary.

Being an athlete was never about proving something about her disability. 'It was about proving something to Mum and Dad. Proving I could be good at sport,' she says. And she's pretty sure if she'd been born without spina bifida she would have still been an athlete for the simple reason it is how you use your natural talent which sets individuals apart. 'I don't think I would have been a runner, perhaps a cyclist. I think I probably would have been as good because to be good as a Paralympian is not just turning up and having a go: you have to have talent and you have to use it,' she explains.

There is absolutely nothing tragic – a word often used by the non-disabled when viewing disability – about Tanni's life or the fact that she uses a wheelchair. 'There is nothing walking would give me that I don't already have in my life. It might mean I could walk up a few back staircases but that's no big deal,' she observes. In fact her view is that a wheelchair gives her greater mobility, not less.

Tanni's long and decorated career successes owe as much to her own approach to training as to natural talent. But that does not mean there were no challenges and irritations along the way. One was a lack of financial parity with non-disabled athletes when races were won. There was prize money and Tanni negotiated her own sponsorship deals. But the figures were incomparable with the rewards non-disabled athletes received. 'I think people imagine you are on £100,000 a year – it was never that,' she says. In fact, she earned significantly more money in the first year after her retirement in 2007 than during many of her competitive years.

There were other niggles, too, such as a lack of representative kit to race in. 'I had leftover Olympic kit for most of my career,' she recalls. In Athens 2004, despite the fact she had already won nine Paralympic gold medals, she was given one racing suit to compete in 11 times over 12 days. Given her demanding schedule, she asked if it might be possible to have another suit. When that seemed difficult, she offered to buy one. 'I was told it was not fair as I could afford to buy kit and there were some on the squad who could not,' she says. So Tanni, who by now was in a much better financial position than many athletes, offered to buy the extra kit needed for the whole squad. 'Suddenly more kit was found,' she adds.

Whether it is because she is in a wheelchair or because she used it with such devastating effect on the track and road, people remember Tanni Grey-Thompson. They also remember what happened that night at the Sports Personality of the Year awards.

Tanni was sitting in the audience next to some swimmers she did not know and having received the Helen Rollason Award, was lost in thought when the countdown to the main prize began. Her mind was drifting off when it was suddenly brought back to reality. 'And in third place, Britain's best-known Paralympian...'

She had come third in the public telephone vote – proof, were it necessary, of how the watching public viewed her achievements. But while second-place heptathlete, Denise Lewis, and winner, Steve Redgrave, could walk from their seats to the stage to pick up their trophies, the BBC had forgotten to put a ramp in place, which meant Tanni was stuck in the audience.

There was an awkward pause before former England captain Alan Shearer stepped off the podium and took the award to where Tanni was sitting. With typical grace, she wasn't angry about what happened. Instead she was thrilled to receive such a prestigious accolade in a year dominated by Redgrave's historic achievement.

It was, though, a defining moment in British Paralympic history. Of course the BBC apologised to her, but it hardly mattered. The public were indignant. Never again would broadcasters be able to cover Paralympic sport or Paralympic athletes without appreciating what they had achieved and how attitudes towards them had changed.

'Outrage at BBC blunder' said the *Evening Standard* headline the next day, while Gordon Neale, then chief executive of Disability Sport, slammed the oversight. 'I think it is disgusting that the BBC of all people should forget to have a ramp fitted to the podium for her,' he said.

In hindsight the episode became a defining moment in the coverage of disability sport and also enhanced Grey-Thompson's profile. Forgetting the ramp that would have allowed Tanni to wheel herself up onto the stage to collect her award while being an unintentional oversight ended up being one of the best things that could have happened for athletes with a disability.

***

And it was a ramp in another country that was to create a boundary-pushing moment for entirely different reasons.

In October 2010, in Delhi, India, Danielle Brown – a young Paralympic star – waved aside her wheelchair and the ramp, deciding instead to step onto the podium to receive her gold medal at the Commonwealth Games in the Team Compound Archery competition. Brown, who uses a wheelchair (though not exclusively), had already made history earlier in the week by becoming the first disabled athlete to represent England in non-disabled competition. Now she'd gone one better, playing her part in winning the team event with fellow archers, Nicky Hunt and Nichola Simpson. Victory in Delhi was a long way from where it all began for Danielle: at Shipton Rugby Club seven years earlier where she started a six-week beginner's course in archery after a chance conversation on the school bus.

Brought up in the tiny village of Lothersdale, Keighley, in north Yorkshire and the eldest of three girls, Danielle loved sport of every kind. It probably helped that her parents, Duncan and Liz, were active and from the sounds of things, pretty hardy.

By the time she was 11, though, for no particular reason Danielle found walking any distance was becoming unbearably painful. Long family walks became an endurance test of pain rather than anything remotely enjoyable.

It was four years and endless doctor and hospital appointments later before specialists at Great Ormond Street Hospital in London finally diagnosed Chronic Regional Pain Syndrome (CRPS), a rare pain condition which can affect any area of the body. In Danielle's case, it was her feet that were affected and causing such discomfort that it was as if they had been placed in a fire and were constantly under attack from sharp, shooting pains. Even at night there was little relief.

CRPS means continuous pain and can be caused either by a simple injury or by a more serious one where nerve damage occurs. It is more common in women and older people, aged 50–70, although it can affect all ages, including children.

By now unable to take part in ordinary everyday sporting activities, Danielle heard about archery on the school bus and wanted to have a go. And so, for her 15th birthday present, she was given an archery course. Every Saturday she would spend three hours learning the basic techniques needed. Although she frequently missed the target – and was, she says, 'terrible' – after years of being stuck indoors unable to do any sport at all, she loved archery right from the start.

Archery is one of the oldest competitive sports of all. Although there are various different forms, target archery (where the aim is to hit a stationary circular target from varying distances) is the most popular. There are both indoor and outdoor competitions.

Archery also has a long Olympic and Paralympic pedigree. It was first introduced as an Olympic sport in 1900 and then dropped in 1908. Reintroduced for a single Games in 1920, it had a 52-year exile before returning in 1972, where it has remained as an Olympic fixture ever since. The most recent British athlete to win a medal at the Olympic

Games is Alison Williamson, who won bronze at Athens 2004. It has been a Paralympic sport at every Games since Rome 1960.

In domestic and international competitions archers can choose to compete with either a recurve or compound bow. At Olympic level, only Recurve competitions exist while at the Paralympic Games, both Recurve and Compound are contested. Recurve features bows that are the modern-day equivalent of the traditional longbow, whereas Compound uses bows that are shorter in length and allow the arrow, once released, to travel faster. They also have pulleys at the end of the limbs and telescopic sights.

Archery targets are 122cm in diameter and archers shoot from a distance of 70m. The gold ring at the centre (which is worth a maximum 10 points) measures 12.2cm. There is absolutely no difference in the targets or distance an archer shoots from in Olympic or Paralympic competition, making this one of the few sports where there is parity between disabled and non-disabled competitors. Apart from a few exceptional cases where the level of disability is extreme, most competitors with a disability use identical equipment to the non-disabled.

The six-week course was a resounding success. Instead of missing out on sport, Danielle had discovered an activity she could do two or three times a week. Within months she'd bought her own secondhand compound bow and soon she was entering archery competitions. It was here that her talent was first spotted by the non-disabled Yorkshire Junior squad, who invited her to join.

In 2005, the 17-year-old won both the indoor and outdoor non-disabled Junior National Championships. By now, though, the pain in her feet was becoming more intense and she was increasingly dependent on crutches to get around. 'I had a lot of pain in my feet but I didn't consider myself disabled,' she says.

When Danielle won the Junior Championships, her winning trophy and medal were presented by John Cavanagh, the British archer who had won gold in the Individual Compound W1 at the Athens 2004 Games. It seemed the perfect moment to ask about the Paralympic Games. He suggested she make contact with Archery GB, the sport's governing body, which she did.

As a result she was invited to attend a Development Squad weekend at Stoke Mandeville. Although Danielle was looking forward to a weekend of shooting practice she didn't realise the get-together would have unexpected, and unseen, benefits: it would change her outlook. 'I didn't know anyone else who was disabled,' she says. She'd already wrestled with the, 'Why is this happening to me?' question but now, in this context, she found herself surrounded by athletes with a disability, many of whom had far more severe disabilities and yet still managed to get around with relative ease. Seeing how other athletes coped so well had a profound impact beyond simple learning and information exchange from others: it helped Danielle accept her disability.

By now she had been offered a place to read a Law degree at Leicester University and before long was also asked to compete for the non-disabled Junior team at the World Championships in Mexico. The experience, Danielle's first long-haul trip, obviously agreed with her as she came fourth.

The following year, she jumped from being fourth in the Junior World Championships to winning the senior Paralympic World Championships in Korea. 'There are no international junior events for disabled archers,' she says. 'My face hurt so much because I didn't stop smiling all night.' Hoping for a top-six finish, winning was beyond anything she expected – and her accuracy was superb. She broke eight world records in the course of the tournament. 'Even now I don't know what happened,' she says. 'I felt I could have stood on my head and pointed the bow in the opposite direction and the arrows would still have hit the target.' According to her head coach, Tim Hazell, one of the characteristics that sets Danielle apart is her accuracy, obviously a critical part of the sport. 'She does not shoot a very orthodox style,' he said, 'but she has an uncanny aiming ability.'

One unexpected benefit of Danielle's ability in archery is the temporary relief from the everyday pain it gives. 'It is still there, but I don't think about it so much. It is a bit of escapism for me,' she explains.

Given her results, selection for the Beijing 2008 Paralympic Games was a near certainty but even so, she didn't want her parents coming with her to China to watch in case seeing them as spectators put her off. However, as they all sat at home watching the Olympic Games on television, she became increasingly nervous at the prospect of being on the same international stage in a few weeks' time without her family support network and so changed her mind, deciding she would like them there after all. By then, though, it was too late to alter plans and buy flights and tickets: Duncan and Liz Brown would have to shout at the television instead.

Although undoubtedly an amazing experience to be a part of, Beijing was also a surreal one which stayed with Danielle even after she had returned. In the Paralympic Village British athletes had to wear the red, white and blue colours in rotation to create a team 'look' and unity.

For days after her return Danielle would wonder whether it was a red, white or blue day. And then there were the endless hours in the Village once the day's training was over, with not much to do. 'There are only so many DVDs you can watch and books you can read,' she says. As a consequence she ended up eating about five meals a day. 'I'm lucky I am not in a sport that requires a certain body weight,' she says. 'I didn't cope with it very well.'

All the same, she made it through to the final with relative ease but then she was worried that, having come all this way, her shooting might let her down on the big day. It helped that her boyfriend, Ali Jawad (a Powerlifter on the British team) sat with her all afternoon and evening reminding her not to doubt her huge ability. She also received an inspirational email from Simon Scott, a professional colleague back in Nottingham, whose archery shop had provided Danielle with all her equipment in the run-up to the competition. 'You can shoot scores in your sleep your competitors can only dream about,' he said. Not that Danielle slept that well the night before the final: she was much too nervous.

The Archery Individual Compound – Open competition was being held at the Paralympic Games for the first time and involved an initial ranking round followed by a series of head-to-heads until two archers were left to fight it out for gold and silver. In the final, Danielle's opponent was Japan's Chieko Kamiya, who managed to progress despite shooting relatively poorly in the ranking round. Since Kamiya was assured a medal of one colour or another, the Japanese media crowded round to get a glimpse of the action. For Danielle, it was only ever about one medal: gold. But for Chieko, it was all about enjoying the moment, savouring the atmosphere and waving to the crowd. At 48 years old it was hard to know how many more opportunities might come Chieko's way and she wanted to make the most of the limelight. Despite the distractions, Danielle needed to keep her concentration. And she did, securing gold with an arrow to spare. Chieko may not have been so demanding or challenging an opponent as she might have expected, but Danielle was now champion of the inaugural Compound Archery – Open competition in the Paralympic Games.

Already her performances were helping to redefine what was possible for Paralympic athletes but that became even more apparent in the Delhi 2010 Commonwealth Games where, just to gain selection, she had to shoot against – and beat – non-disabled archers. And while winning in Delhi attracted huge media interest, competing against non-disabled competitors is entirely normal for Danielle. The only difference is, she uses a stool to shoot from because her balance is so poor. Anyone watching that October day at the Yamuna Sports Complex in Delhi would have seen a display of poise, skill, self-belief and extraordinary mental tenacity under immense pressure. When an athlete rises to the occasion and delivers on a global stage, this is elite sport at its very best, disabled or not.

While Danielle Brown made history in Delhi this is not a feat that can be repeated at London 2012. Her event, Individual Compound, is on the Paralympic but not the Olympic programme, ruling out a triumphant Indian re-run. But London 2012 or not, Danielle has already pushed the parameters of her sport to new limits.

***

Defining moments are often about extraordinary sporting achievements that raise competition, and spectator experience, to a new level. Like the day in Beijing 2008, when Chris Hoy did something no other British athlete, from any sport, has done for 100 years by becoming the first Olympian since swimmer Henry Taylor in 1908 to win three gold medals at a single Games. These are the once-in-a-generation, thrilling sporting moments people talk about for years to come. And they are the images we see replayed time and again on our screens afterwards.

When South Africa's Natalie du Toit removed her prosthetic limb, dived off the pontoon and into Beijing's Shunyi Lake on 20 August 2008 for the start of the Marathon Swimming 10km she joined an elite band of Paralympic athletes who have crossed the divide between Olympic Games and Paralympic Games participation.

Alongside 24 of the best open-water swimmers in the world, du Toit more than held her own despite the disadvantage of swimming 10km with just one leg, in a sport which requires the kicking action of both. She finished 16th, just 1 minute and 22 seconds behind the eventual winner, Larisa Ilchenko of Russia, after an event which demands almost two hours of non-stop effort. For Natalie it was the fulfilment of a lifetime's dream and made her the first female amputee to compete in an Olympic event. To date only five athletes, including du Toit, have competed at both Paralympic and Olympic level in the Summer Games. All have been women. Two competed in Archery, one in Athletics and another in Table Tennis. None have won a medal.

So far no British athlete has competed at both Games, although as Danielle Brown has shown, there are those already good enough to take on the best in the world in non-disabled sport and win.

Another athlete good enough to take on non-disabled competition is Sarah Storey, who faces a boundary pushing moment of her own in the run-up to the London Games. Storey could become the first British athlete, and the first cyclist, to cross the threshold from Paralympic athlete to Olympic athlete.

Like Jody Cundy, a fellow member of the GB Paralympic Cycling team, Storey has already enjoyed a swimming career that's the envy of many, winning five gold medals in four Games from Barcelona 1992 to Athens 2004. London 2012 will be her sixth Games. 'I'm almost the grandma of the team,' she says. Well, hardly. When London 2012 comes around, she'll be 34. But it's in the Velodrome that she's attracted unprecedented media interest because of the possibility that she might compete at both Paralympic and Olympic Games.

Born in Manchester but brought up in Disley, on the edge of the Peak District, Sarah – the eldest of three children – loved all sport. It helped that her younger brother and sister were also gifted and talented athletes, going on to participate at national level in their own events. Competing was very much a family affair. 'We would spend hours in the car here, there and everywhere,' she explains. 'The reason I am where I am physically is the way my parents brought me up.'

Although born with a deformed left hand, her parents never treated her any differently so there was nothing to stop her from fulfilling her dreams and ambitions. Besides, her own grandmother worked with the profoundly disabled and as far as she was concerned, Sarah was very well-off indeed.

At the age of six she watched the Los Angeles 1984 Olympic Games and decided there and then that she wanted to become an athlete. To her the particular sport that would eventually involve was less important than the eventual outcome.

So she played on the boys' cricket team for a while, enjoyed netball, ran for her county, swam and was a table-tennis champion. But it was, she says, swimming which 'chose' her and first gave her the chance to internationally compete for her country.

At 14, Sarah Storey attended her first Paralympic Games in Barcelona 1992, where she won two gold medals. By the time Atlanta 1996 was over, still aged only 18, she had five. Two came in the 200m Individual Medley SM10, where swimmers do all four strokes – Butterfly, Backstroke, Breaststroke and Freestyle – proving she really was the master of multi-events.

And she kept very good training company, joining Stockport Metro Swimming Club, one of the country's top clubs. Day in, day out she would spend hours completing the mileage required alongside swimmers like Graeme Smith, who won a bronze medal in the gruelling 1500m Freestyle, in Atlanta. Just like Danielle Brown's archery career, Sarah Storey has regularly trained, and raced, alongside non-disabled athletes.

After Athens 2004, recurring ear infections made pool training increasingly difficult. Not wanting to do too much running in case of leg injury, Sarah went out on a bike to stay fit. 'I didn't realise I would be as good as I turned out to be,' she says, as she quickly became a world record holder on the track and a multiple European champion.

There would be no more 5am training sessions as Sarah swapped the pool for pedals and on average, three to six hour's cycling a day, which could rise to seven or eight hours during intense periods. With a winter track season and summer road competitions to prepare for, training can be all-consuming for cyclists.

When she married her husband Barney, who she met at a competition, they planned it around the cycling season. Like so many other top athletes, this was not a sacrifice: sporting events are immovable and the opportunity to do something others cannot, rare.

Although her parents never dwelt on why Sarah had a different left hand to her siblings, her mother once said, 'If only I could give you my hand.' To which Sarah replied, 'You'd be useless with one!' Sarah has learnt to be dextrous and although not having a fully formed hand does affect the pull required at the start of a race, she's developed techniques to overcome this so she can race on equal terms with the female endurance riders. 'Once we are up to speed, there is no difference,' she says.

All of which paid dividends at Beijing 2008, when Storey won double gold in the Time Trial and the Pursuit (both C1-2/CP4 category), where she set a new world-record time – and all this from someone who'd only been cycling for three years. Her Beijing experience was made even sweeter because Barney won gold on the same day when he rode as the pilot in the Sprint B VI 1–3 for his partially-sighted teammate, Anthony Kappes.

Even then, Storey was already knocking on the door of the Olympic Games. Her world record time in Beijing would have been good enough to finish sixth in the Olympic Games in the event won by compatriot Rebecca Romero. Like Storey, Romero had switched from being a high performer in one sport – she won silver as a rower in the Quadruple Scull (4x) at Athens 2004 – to go one better at Beijing 2008 in a completely different one.

If a seed had been sown in Beijing it would well and truly take root when, in December 2009, the IOC ratified changes to the Olympic Games programme for 2012 proposed by the sport's governing body, the International Cycling Union (UCI). In Beijing the men contested seven events, the women three; in London, in order to increase women's participation on the track, there will be five events for each. One of the new female additions will be the Team Pursuit. Made up of three riders, this is the event Sarah Storey has her eyes on as it is one not featured on the Paralympic programme.

Rather than get caught up in the 'what ifs', Storey sees the new event as a chance to add something to her programme which will enhance the existing work she is already doing. 'I am focusing on events,' she says. 'Creating history is an outcome that might happen, it might not.'

As someone who has competed in multiple events in the pool at previous Games, this seems a natural progression. Nevertheless, the road from Paralympic superstar to Olympic start line is littered with twists and turns. One of the biggest hurdles lies right on her doorstep in the shape of the British team itself, which is one of the strongest in the world. Such is the strength in depth Sarah must first contend with the likes of Romero (Olympic Individual Pursuit champion), Wendy Houvenaghel (Olympic and Commonwealth Individual Pursuit silver medallist), Lizzie Armitstead (World Champion in Team Pursuit) and some highly rated junior riders including Laura Trott and Dani King, just to make the team.

However, Storey proved she could more than hold her own in this company when, together with Wendy Houvenaghel and Joanna Rowsell, she finished just a quarter of a second outside the world record when they won the Team Pursuit on the opening day of the Manchester Track World Cup in February 2011. Apart from the exhilaration of winning in such a fast time the event gave a hint of what the London 2012 Games will offer. 'Racing in front of the Manchester crowd was an insight into next year in London,' says Sarah. She did wonder what all the noise was while racing, though. 'They sound like they are inside my aero helmet,' she adds.

Like Danielle Brown, Sarah made her own piece of history in Delhi the October before when she became the first Paralympic cyclist to compete against non-disabled athletes at the Commonwealth Games.

The stories of Danielle Brown and Sarah Storey emphasise, if such emphasis is needed, how exceptionally talented world-beaters compete in Paralympic sport today. Danielle's event is not featured in the Olympic Games, so she cannot cross the divide, leaving the focus and media pressure on Sarah Storey. But whatever happens between now and when the final selection is made, Paralympic sport is not about making comparisons. 'I think if an athlete is capable of competing in both, that is great,' observed Baroness Sue Campbell, Chair of UK Sport, 'but we should judge the Paralympic Games for what it is, which is world-class athletes who have a disability. If some make the bridge across, then fantastic, but I don't think we should see that as better or worse.'

It's certainly a view shared by Sarah Storey, who believes athletes who compete in the Paralympic Games are simply athletes who, through circumstance, have disabilities; the only difference is in the function of the limbs. It's also a common misconception that athletes in the Paralympic Games have to try harder than athletes in the Olympic Games. 'The option of doing the Olympic Games only came about because I have an event at those Games that isn't available to me at the Paralympics,' she says.

In sport, reaching an Olympic or Paralympic Games is the goal all athletes strive for. To do so in one sport and win medals is inspirational enough. To achieve that in two as well as to strive to compete against non-disabled competition leaves its own mark no matter who is finally named in the British Olympic Cycling team for London 2012. Storey's journey has shone a bright light on Paralympic Cycling and shown, whether now or in the near future, for Sarah or another rider of her calibre, the moment will surely come when a Paralympic cyclist clips into their pedals alongside an Olympic one. History really does beckon.

Chapter Eight

On Top of the World

**'Not in the clamour of the crowded street,
not in the shouts and plaudits of the throng,
but in ourselves our triumph and defeat.'**

Henry Longfellow, poet

Anybody who watches an event like the Paralympic Games will have a raft of questions they need answering. It doesn't much matter whether the athlete is disabled or non-disabled, the enquiries are usually still the same. What does it take to win on one of the world's biggest sporting stages? What's it like to have years of hard work, dedication and physical stress come down to a single performance in an athlete's life? How does it feel to go from having a few spectators turn up to watch your event one week to performing in front of thousands of cheering, autograph-seeking fans in state-of-the-art venues the next, when there is not a spare seat in the house?

And what's it like to do the one thing athletes the world over dream about day in, day out? To deliver the performance of a lifetime when it really counts and then to alight onto the highest step of the most famous multi-sport podium in the world, a gold medal dangling round your neck, to hear the national anthem played in honour of your achievement and the moment. What's it like to win a televised global event and know the word 'champion' will be forever associated with your name?

In fact athletes react differently to success and what viewers see on their television screens is only a small part of the story.

***

Lee Pearson has nine Paralympic gold medals to date. He is the most successful Paralympic Games rider in the world and remains unbeaten in any Paralympic competition since his first win at Sydney 2000. He's been awarded an MBE, OBE and CBE in recognition of his achievements and visited Buckingham Palace more often than he's bought horses – seven invites so far. He once, famously, offered to give HM the Queen a riding lesson, should she ever find herself passing through Staffordshire to which, allegedly, she replied by saying she might just take him up on the offer.

He's sung live on BBC television to raise funds for Sport Relief, been immortalised in a special bronze statue to commemorate the Games, talked openly about being gay and how the news at first shocked his family, and been invited to a string of award ceremonies and celebrity parties. Lee is one of the best-known faces of today's Paralympic athletes. Yet despite being in the limelight, he feels nothing but terror every time a Paralympic Games approaches. As the medals and titles have racked up too, so has the expectation of winning. And no one puts so much pressure on Lee Pearson as he puts on himself.

At Sydney 2000 few had ever heard of Lee when he won the first of nine gold medals. In London, the pressure on him will be immense as he goes for another clutch of golds. But then Pearson loves being in the top spot. He's not involved in a sport which puts a huge strain on his body to travel the world or collect another Paralympic participation medal: he's in it to win and to remain the number one Paralympic rider in the world. No more, no less.

Surprisingly perhaps, considering he's the best in the world at what he does and has entered (and won) non-disabled competitions, there are many days when he thinks he can't ride at all. 'Horses never allow you to think you are any good: they can make you feel the best person on the planet one day and that you couldn't ride one end of a broomstick the next day,' he explains.

And such are his pre-Games nerves, he can't even bear to watch his horses being bathed, plaited and tacked up in the hours before the Dressage events begin. Instead he must take himself off to another part of the venue to get away. And he's only happy to watch others competing if they are riding in a different classification to his, otherwise he decides his direct competitors look better than he does.

So, while others prepare his horse Lee gets changed and then once he's ready, he spends the last few moments making final adjustments and calming his frayed nerves before the serious work begins. Unlike other sports, he never forgets he is competing with an animal in an environment where anything can, and does, happen. And while he knows the significance of the next few moments and how they could change his life, the horse may have other ideas.

Once the bell sounds to signal the start of the competition, it's a question of total application and concentration on the job in hand. In Lee's case, as he usually competes in both team and individual events, he has three competitive Dressage Tests to complete – the Team, Championship and Freestyle Tests.

Lee Pearson has an engaging and entertaining personality, so it's hard to imagine him doing clerical work in a backroom at a supermarket in Staffordshire while on Prozac to keep his feelings of depression at bay. Yet that was his life as a young man, disillusioned by his disability and the lack of opportunity open to him because of it.

As is so often the case, life-changing events are all about timing. Who knows how long he would have tolerated his former life had he not, in 1996, been sitting at home in Cheddleton, Staffordshire, watching the Atlanta Paralympic Games? As he looked on, he thought: I can do that. So he rang the RDA and with typical directness, told them he'd like to be part of the Great Britain team competing at the Sydney 2000 Games in four years' time.

Whether they thought he was joking or not, someone was sent to assess Pearson's condition and as he rode around the field at the back of where his parents lived, they could hardly believe what they were seeing. And Lee Pearson couldn't quite take in what they were saying. 'They told me I was really disabled,' he says. And yet, as far as he was concerned, he had always led a pretty mainstream life, driving his car, holding down a job and going clubbing.

With his classification established as the most severe on the then classification scale, Pearson began dressage the following year, in 1997. The office job he found so limiting was no more. Not that riding was a particularly electrifying experience to start with. 'The first couple of years were so boring,' he explained. 'It would be a bit like me asking you to do gymnastics on the floor. It's all about improving balance and power, and until you improve those skills, it is a bit dull. But as you learn to do more, it becomes more interesting and then suddenly, you get the bug.' And what a bug it turned out to be. From his first Games in Sydney to his most recent in Beijing, Lee Pearson has won every Paralympic event he's entered and there are not many athletes who can say that about their career.

Like all great athletes, he puts his success down to a number of factors. For a start, he works hard at a daily routine which involves riding three horses in a specially constructed arena, complete with mirrors so he can check his movements, in his yard. But if he rides too much, he runs the risk of being in severe pain the following day because of the extent of his disability.

He also has an uncanny ability to bring out the best in the horses he works with: exceptional balance, an understanding of what a horse can feel from the rider and what is needed to get a response. 'Able-bodied people over-use their limbs,' he explains. 'I can't kick a horse hard, so I have to make them respond to a light kick. It's enough – a horse can feel a fly on it.'

And there's another ingredient central to his success: resourcefulness. His house has none of the adaptations you'd expect for someone who is not very tall. There are no cupboards fixed at low heights so he can reach them. Instead he places a cushion on the floor to create a landing pad for items he needs and uses one of his crutches to pull down the can of beans or whatever else he requires, hoping they land safely in the designated spot.

Like many disabled people he's learnt to be adaptable and not to accept the view of those who only see what cannot be done rather than what can. 'We don't need someone to come along and say you can't do that – we know what we can do,' he says, adding, 'I have been problem solving all my life.' Indeed, being adaptable is an essential skill to master the different personalities of each of the horses he rides.

But when the Paralympic event is finally over, the tack packed away and the long hours of hard, repetitive work have been rewarded with the knowledge that a gold medal will soon be hanging around his neck, what does Lee savour most? Is this a moment of pure pleasure and utter relief? Or a chance to soak up the atmosphere and watch the distinctive red, white and blue flag rise to the top of the pole accompanied by an anthem that must mean more to him than most after so many meetings with the Monarch?

Perhaps surprisingly, victory is not the time when Lee can let the emotions go and wave joyfully to his friends and family while simultaneously grinning at photographers, media pundits and cameramen. It's anything but that. The immediate moments after winning at the Paralympic Games are neither as relaxing nor so enjoyable as one might think: he's emotionally and physically exhausted, and the last thing he wants to do is get back on his horse for a mounted ceremony, which is when riders receive their medals on horseback.

While others wrap themselves in the Union Jack flag, do a lap of honour or embrace their nearest and dearest, elite horsemen and women have other responsibilities to tend to. 'I'm sitting on a live animal,' he explains. 'You really want people to cheer but the problem you have is, will your horse freak out if everyone does that?'

And will the horse dutifully comply and move forward just as the dignitary of the day appears to present the medals, or will it become overly excited by the noise, the clapping, cheering and endless camera flashes and ruin the presentation for the rider and everyone else? 'I am still in work mode,' Lee says, 'so I can't relax.' Added to that is the hidden reality that sitting motionless on a horse creates constant, grating pain for him, which only moving around will alleviate. When it's a mounted ceremony, moving just isn't possible until it's over.

After hours spent perfecting the smallest movement, years of dedicated training in an outdoor ring regardless of the weather, endless time spent planning and competing in build-up competitions to qualify and prepare the horse, and then days of high anxiety in the run-up to the Paralympic Games, the celebrations for these magical moments in Lee Pearson's life have to wait just that bit longer.

***

While Lee Pearson was coming to terms with victory during one part of Athens 2004, across town, at the Olympic Stadium, Tanni Grey-Thompson was having no trouble at all in celebrating her first victory of the Games.

Although more than two-and-a-half years would pass before she officially retired at the Paralympic World Cup in Manchester, in May 2007, Tanni already knew this – her fifth Games – would be her last. There would be no Beijing in 2008 for her.

Coming into the Games the 35-year-old was in terrific shape and racing in the build-up had gone better than expected, as she told the BBC in August 2004: 'I broke the 200m world record this year, I broke the 400m world record and I did a personal best in the 800m earlier on to qualify to be in the Paralympics, and I did a personal best in the 100m. So I'm racing the fastest I've ever done – whether it's quick enough, I don't know,' she said. 'I'll find out in three weeks' time, but the way I'm pushing right now, I'm really pleased.'

Ever since her student days at Loughborough, Tanni had sought ways to outsmart her rivals when it came to training. Before the Seoul 1988 Games, she'd used a heat chamber to ensure her body was prepared for the heat and humidity of South Korea. And in 1993, more than a decade before the Athens 2004 Games, she had approached the distinguished Australian wheelchair coach, Jenni Banks, and asked if she could join her coaching group in Australia for three-and-a-half months. When she returned to England, she continued to be coached by Banks until 1996 and although Ian Thompson, her husband, became increasingly involved after 1997. Banks' influence would last for the remainder of her career.

Tanni arrived in Greece in great shape and was looking forward to defending the four titles won at Sydney 2000 – 100m, 200m, 400m and 800m but she didn't begin well at all. In her first event, the 800m, she only finished seventh. 'The 800m was so bad,' she says. 'I was really flat, there was no energy or speed and lots of things went wrong.'

Unused to losing, it was a defeat she took particularly badly. 'After the 800m I wasn't the most sociable person on the team,' she admits. But if she wanted to lick her wounds in private, teammates and compatriots had other ideas. 'What was hard was the number of people who came up to me and said to me, "Are you alright?" That was really emotional. If you won, you might get a few people saying well done. It was really hard, people saying, "I am really sorry to hear about the race." People were being so nice. It would have been better if they had ignored me,' she says.

Against this backdrop, she arrived at the Olympic Stadium for the 100m final, a race which, after four years of preparation, would be over in less than 20 seconds. Throughout her career Tanni had struggled with pre-race nerves, something that became worse as she grew older. She was used to being sick before the start of the London Marathon and prior to track races, but at the Athens 2004 Games she threw up 12 times during the warm-up. And she was still retching as she went across the warm-up track to enter the call room, where athletes wait in the moments before the countdown to their final begins.

The athletes were led onto the track by officials. It was a little before 6pm. The race start time was 1803. Tanni just sat there, shaking and looking at the clock as it moved, like a hedgehog, from 1800 to 1801 and then to 1802. Finally, the clock reached 1803 and the race was on. Even now she still recalls all of the 17.24 seconds it took from start to finishing line. For Tanni, it unfolded in super-slow motion. 'I remember every push of the race,' she says.

Well down at 30m, she could see the Italian, Francesca Porcellato, at least a chair-length ahead. 'She got an amazing start,' Tanni says. As she pushed her wheelchair towards the advancing Italian, no noise entered her periphery, no distraction could be countenanced as every sinew, nerve and muscle concentrated on pushing closer and closer to Porcellato until, at 55m, they drew level. At 60m, Tanni edged ahead. By 80m, the finishing line was within touching distance. At 100m, she had won the 10th Paralympic gold medal of her career and the silence in her head erupted into screams and cheers, which she could now hear. 'Technically, it was one of the best races I have ever done,' she admits. 'It was really emotional for me.'

And although she would go on to win an historic 11th gold medal in the 400m a few days later, this is still the race, more than any other in her career, she remembers the most.

After the 800m that she wanted to forget, the only emotion Grey-Thompson felt was relief. 'I desperately didn't want to have another bad race,' she says. 'I don't care about the time: I could have done 25 seconds and it wouldn't have mattered as long as I won the gold medal.'

What did matter, though, in the immediate moments after winning, was looking into the crowd to spot her two-and-a-half-year-old daughter, Carys, wearing a 'Go Mammy' T-shirt. It didn't take long to locate the familiar figure of the toddler in the stands. Carys was eating an ice cream and she had absolutely no interest in the significance of what her mother had just achieved. 'She barely watched it,' Tanni says. 'She just wasn't at all bothered.' And yet Carys Grey-Thompson might not have been at the Athens 2004 Games at all – Tanni's training schedule was so packed after Sydney 2000 that there was little time to think about starting a family.

***

Tanni Grey-Thompson only raced to win. Being born with spina bifida was an irrelevance, a lens through which others looked and, perhaps, judged her. It was never the way she viewed herself. During her career, significant life events were meticulously planned and managed so as not to interfere with her chances of elite success. As any athlete will tell you, a career at the top, is often all too short. There's no time to miss out on golden opportunities. 'Our wedding in 1999 was based around our competition schedule,' Tanni says. 'There were two days that year we could get married, because of our joint racing commitments.'

In fact the date she and her husband-to-be chose happened to coincide with a track race and initially, Tanni and Ian, considered racing in the morning and then getting to the church in time for an afternoon ceremony, much to the horror of Sulwen Grey, Tanni's mother.

In the end the race was cancelled, but Tanni still got up in time to go training at 7am (the wedding was at 2pm). Sulwen knew she was never going to change her daughter, so as Tanni set off for her five-mile training circuit around the streets of Cardiff, she issued an ultimatum. 'Do not crash your chair, do not get a black eye and do not fall out! Understand? If you do, I will never speak to you again.' And Tanni obeyed.

In 2001, a year after the Sydney 2000 Games and three years before the Athens 2004 Games, there was, says Tanni, 'an eight-week window to get pregnant that year. If I had not fallen pregnant, we would have waited until after Athens,' she adds.

Tanni and Ian had thought Carys would arrive in mid-January 2002. In fact, she was born in early February, which meant less time than Tanni anticipated to get back into shape for the 2002 London Marathon, at which, for the sixth and final time of her career, she crossed the line as the winner.

When Carys was just two weeks old her mother went to Spain for a training camp. A week later, she did a half-Marathon and then, when Carys was seven weeks old, a 10k race. Just nine weeks after giving birth, Tanni lined up for the London Marathon and won. After the race, she found blood in her urine and went to seek medical help from the St John

Ambulance team. When she told them she was passing blood, she was advised not to worry as it happened to a lot of women after such physical exertion. So she explained she'd had minor surgery a few weeks back.

When asked what the surgery was she explained it was a caesarian to which she was asked how long ago it had taken place. When Tanni explained only nine weeks and six days had passed the volunteer misheard and said as 10 months had gone by, there was nothing to worry about. When Tanni explained it was less than 10 weeks, not 10 months, a mild panic ensued and a doctor was called for, who promptly admonished her. 'Are you just stupid thinking you can do a Marathon nine weeks after a caesarian?' he said.

For Tanni, racing in London so soon after Carys' arrival was an easy decision. 'That is what you do,' she says, adding, 'If you are going to do something you do it properly.' Still, it might have been a welcome sight if, at Athens 2004, Carys had looked up from her ice cream for just a second.

Throughout her career, Grey-Thompson's motivation, was to beat the best athletes in the world. If achieving this meant doing things others believed foolhardy, so be it. She wouldn't change a thing.

A few days after her 100m victory at Athens 2004, Tanni won the 400m, her second win of the Games and taking her all-time tally to 11 gold medals. This figure may be eclipsed at London 2012, as swimmer Dave Roberts took his total number of gold medals to 11 at Beijing 2008. At the Athens 2004 Games, however, it made Tanni Grey-Thompson Britain's most successful British Paralympic athlete and you don't get to that milestone without a lifetime's dedication, professionalism and commitment.

Even her retirement date was changed because illness prevented her from being at her best and she wanted to retire on her terms, not anyone else's. The plan was to finish at the World Championships in Assen, in the Netherlands, in September 2006, but the build-up didn't go according to plan. 'I went to the World Championships and got gold, silver and bronze, but didn't feel I did myself justice,' she reveals. 'Not winning when you have done everything possible I can accept, but I came away thinking that wasn't me doing my best.'

Instead she decided to finish in front of an appreciative home crowd the following May, when her father, sister and close friends could all be there to help celebrate the end of a glittering track and road career.

When Tanni Grey-Thompson eventually retired, at the age of 37, she left Paralympic sport in a more robust place in the public's perception than when she had started at Seoul 1988. Her attitude and desire to win, her dominance on the track and road, and willingness to engage with the public in a compelling way played, in no small measure, a big part in this change.

***

As Tanni Grey-Thompson was enjoying the deserved attention and plaudits that followed her 11th Paralympic medal, another British athlete made his own piece of history with the same ruthless, meticulous approach to winning.

When Peter Norfolk left the players' entrance at the Athens Olympic Tennis Centre to meet the USA's David Wagner in the Quad Singles final, he knew what happened next was up to him.

More than a decade after being paralysed in a motorbike accident, he's always loved the cat-and-mouse attributes of a game which differs little in strategy from the standing-up version. And he knows if it doesn't work out, there is only one person to point the finger of blame at. 'There is nowhere to hide. If I lose, I can't blame you,' he says. 'I am the one on court – I have to find any way I can to win.'

And at the Athens 2004 Paralympic Games, at 43, an age when many athletes have retired, Peter Norfolk won his first Paralympic gold medal. What's more, he knew from various points won during the match what the final outcome would be. 'I remember hitting the last shot and as soon as the ball left my racquet, I knew I had won. There were earlier points when I knew I was going to win, but I still had to focus,' he says.

Victory in Athens 2004 was a bittersweet experience though – his wife Linda, the team's physiotherapist, lost their first baby back in England following the Games. There were other happier memories, however, such as looking up into the crowd whenever he hit a winning shot and seeing everyone screaming and clapping, including blind members of the British Judo team who had come to support him – it was just that they were looking in the opposite direction to where he'd placed his shot and where everyone else was looking!

Once it was all over and the gold medal secured, he felt immense, overwhelming relief. 'To put in place a plan and then action it for four years and achieve those goals is astounding,' he says. Together with another friend, Peter and Linda waited until all the lights had gone out and everyone had left before having their own victory party outside the stadium. And then they made their way onto the last bus back to the Village.

At every Paralympic Games inevitably there are situations and experiences that can unsettle young and experienced competitors if they allow them to do so. None more so than the glitzy celebrations that usually mark the Opening and Closing Ceremonies of each Games. At Athens 2004 Philip Craven, President of the International Paralympic Committee and himself a distinguished former wheelchair basketball player, told the crowd: 'More than 2,000 years ago, the Greek philosopher Democritos said, "To win oneself is the first and best of all victories." This holds true for all athletes but especially for Paralympians.' It's all part of the grand introduction to the Games, along with the light shows, dancers and fireworks.

But although these ceremonies are great spectacles, often they are also long, tiring and distracting if an athlete's sole aim is to win gold. Athletes such as Peter Norfolk don't train or compete for the Ceremonies or post-Games parade through the streets of the capital. For Peter, and athletes like him, it's all about the prize of gold. 'I am not interested in it,' he explains. 'I have got what I want, and that's the medal; I have been on the podium. For me, the fight was the match as I only play to win. You only remember the winners.'

Such is his approach that, at the big events like the Paralympic Games, he is totally absorbed and focused on doing the job he's come for. As he prepares for the biggest Games of his career, he has certain pre-match rituals that help him prepare.

'I do go into my cave a bit as I'm not interested in anything except the next game,' he admits. In fact, Peter is a master in knowing what works for him and how to shut out the rest of the world and let the winning ways in. It's a well-practised and well-trodden route which has seen him secure more than 40 Quad singles titles on the Wheelchair Tennis Tour. He also won the US Open at Flushing Meadows twice and the Australian Open, in Melbourne, three times. Until 2010 he finished as Number 1 in the Quad world rankings in five of the previous seven seasons.

Four years after the Athens Games, Peter arrived at Beijing 2008 to defend his Quad title. In Beijing he didn't drop a single set and progressed without difficulty to the final against Sweden's Johan Andersson. He knew he had to come out strongly: he broke Andersson's serve early in the first set and never looked back, taking his second successive Paralympic Quad title, 6-2, 6-2, after a little more than an hour on court. It was only once he realised he could win that he was able to enjoy the stadium and the crowd, and to soak up the euphoria more than he had at Athens 2004.

For Peter, one of the best experiences of Beijing was the crowd support and when he went to practise on the morning of his final, the stadium was packed with enthusiastic Chinese supporters, who clapped and cheered every point. So, when the session came to an end the players rewarded the enthusiastic support by throwing balls and towels into the crowd. It wasn't an experience or opportunity that comes round often in a player's career and Peter couldn't imagine it getting any better. However, the atmosphere, crowds and support in the final were quite unlike anything he'd ever experienced.

And now, with two Quad titles already under his belt, he has his eyes on London 2012, where he could win both Quad Singles and Doubles with possible partner Andy Lapthorne, who he describes as, 'the future of tennis'.

He intends to adopt exactly the same build-up as for previous Games. 'I want my third gold at London,' he says. 'It is a job. You have got one crack at it, and that's it. There are no second chances, particularly in London. It won't come back round in my lifetime.'

***

Danielle Brown may be nearly 30 years Peter Norfolk's junior but she shares an aim as unerring as her shooting skills: the desire to win. The Frenchman and founder of the modern Olympic Games, Baron Pierre de Coubertin, believed it was not winning that mattered, but the taking part. 'The essential thing in life is not conquering but fighting well,' he said. This may not be a view shared by today's elite Paralympic athletes: participation may be important, but winning is everything.

So much so that the thought of repeating her Beijing success in London 2012 is all the incentive Danielle Brown needs. She hates getting up early. Whether it's the constant pain in her feet caused by CRPS, or that she simply prefers to avoid early starts, Danielle is not at her best first thing.

And yet the only motivation needed to overcome this difficulty is the simple reminder that while she's in bed, somewhere in another part of the world, one of her London 2012 competitors will already be putting that day's training plan into practice. 'I really want to win,' she says. 'It gets me out of bed.'

And when she did win in Beijing there were no words sufficiently adequate to describe what it felt like. Instead she stood shaking from the adrenaline of the moment and the relief it was all over. She was so excited that when the Union Jack went up, after being presented with her medal, she forgot to sing. And once the ceremony was over, all she wanted to do was call home to share the moment with her parents and two younger sisters in Lothersdale, Keighley in north Yorkshire. It was 2.45 in the morning when Helen answered. Having relayed the news that Danielle Brown was now the best Individual Compound – Open archer in the Paralympic world, Helen responded by saying, 'Well done. I've got my university accommodation sorted out.' So, not much danger there of the success going to her head.

Her mother, Liz, though, was jubilant. Danielle hadn't been able to speak to her father, Duncan, who was away on business and so she rang him on his mobile, not realising Liz had already relayed the news. 'Why are you whispering?' she asked him. In fact, it was the second time in as many minutes his room mates had been woken by the phone ringing. It was worth it, though. 'He was chuffed to bits,' she says.

What happened in the months that followed her triumph shows just how big the gulf between non-disabled and disabled sport still is.

Danielle began contacting bow manufacturers to see if she could get sponsorship. None were forthcoming but the minute she qualified for the non-disabled team to compete at the Commonwealth Games in Delhi, suddenly they wanted to support her. And therein lies one of the issues surrounding the Paralympic Games: it's a fact of life that it is still harder, and the opportunities fewer, for someone in a wheelchair than not.

The forerunner to today's Paralympic Games may well have provided the disabled with hope and unexpected opportunity. Today, though, the Paralympic Games are elite sport at their very best, packed with outstanding athletes who achieve remarkable sporting feats in their particular sport. And those athletes do not define their sporting capabilities by their disability. Instead they look at the task in hand – to be the best they can – and set about achieving it. Athletes like Danielle Brown refuse to fall within the preconceived boundaries set by society. Instead they set boundaries of their own.

Understanding this, and Paralympic sport in general, still requires better information so that everyone can fully understand and appreciate the spectacle unfolding in front of them. And that is because watching Paralympic sport is a different experience to watching Olympic events or, indeed, any non-disabled sport. Broadcasting is one of the areas where that understanding can be helped and the broadcaster charged with getting that experience across is the Channel 4, who secured the rights to show the London 2012 Paralympic Games. Under the agreement, Channel 4 has to broadcast 150 hours of coverage during the Games itself as well as commission two 10-part documentaries. Most of the coverage will be live and more than 130 of the 150 hours will be shown on Channel 4's main terrestrial channel. The Games will be the biggest event in Channel 4's history.

Chris Holmes, Director of Paralympic Integration at the London 2012 Organising Committee and himself a winner of six gold medals at one Games, Barcelona 1992, saw the Channel 4 coup as a major highlight of his tenure. 'It was a fantastic deal and really allows us a tremendous opportunity to do something amazing, ensuring people get immersed in Paralympic sport and fall in love with it,' he said.

***

Athens 2004 was the first Games Baroness Sue Campbell attended as Reform Chair of UK Sport. Initially appointed for an 18-month term in September 2003, she was confirmed as UK Sport's Chair for another four years in March 2009, which will see her in office until 2013, beyond the London 2012 Games.

One night, together with John Scott (then International Director and Director of Drug-Free Sport at UK Sport and since Chief Executive of the Glasgow 2014 Commonwealth Games), they decided to make their way over to the Olympic pool. Despite a long involvement with sport of all kinds, nothing quite prepared Campbell for what happened that evening in Greece.

Settling back to watch the most severe category of swimmers, the S1 group, Baroness Campbell looked on as the swimmers paraded along the side of the pool before taking up position behind the lane they were about to swim in. Then one competitor removed both arms, followed by her legs, before getting into the water and using her trunk to propel her, like a fish, to the other end where, rather than touching the wall with an outstretched arm to finish, she used the crown of her head instead.

Up in the stands tears were pouring down Campbell's face. 'John turned to me and said, "What is the matter with you?"' she recalls. 'I am going to go away and be a better person,' she replied. 'It just had that profound effect on me. You don't feel that when you are watching the Olympics – you are enthralled by Paralympic sport. It's magnificent in a different way.'

She believes that if you watch the Paralympic Games and it does not affect or move you, and you don't go away determined to do better with your own life, then you really haven't watched it at all.

Chapter Eight

But that's the thing about the Paralympic Games. Whether it was the pioneers of 1960, stars like rower Tom Aggar and archer Danielle Brown, or athletes who will come into their own for the first time at London 2012, watching Paralympic sport is about recognising and appreciating something that lies within every one of us. It's about the irrepressible power of the human spirit at its very finest and it's simply that in the course of our everyday lives, most of us never have cause to dig that deep for so long to emerge triumphant. That is what the Paralympic Games, past and present, are all about.

Acknowledgements

Writing a book on the Paralympic Games in the very short period of time available to me meant relying on the expertise and experience of a raft of people, without whom this project wouldn't have progressed much beyond the starting blocks. I am grateful to all.

I should say, from the outset, there is a paucity of reliable, accurate information on the Paralympic Games, particularly the early history, which meant relying on the memories of those who experienced the Games first hand rather than any historical documents. And yet decades have passed since those inaugural Games and memories inevitably fade. What is recorded here reflects those remembrances and if there are any inaccuracies, I apologise in advance. The interviews were conducted, and written, in good faith.

In terms of those who made the book happen, thanks first of all to Conor Kilgallon, Senior Editor of Carlton Books, for asking me to write it and for calmly and professionally navigating me through the process and the unexpected, at times challenging, curveballs neither of us could have anticipated in advance.

Thank you also to Nicky Gyopari for reading the original manuscript and for coming up with valuable suggestions.

Acknowledgements

Getting to the finish line would not have been possible without the tenacious, gracious intervention of Ann Cutcliffe (Vice-Chair ParalympicsGB), who opened doors I could not. In the five-month process no one did more to facilitate interviews and ideas. Without her this book would have been poorer in content, understanding and range, and I am indebted for the tireless, enlightened support generously given throughout.

Thanks also to Mel, a good friend and brilliant PR professional, for an invaluable part in the book's inception. and to the incomparable Jane Goldsmith for excellent help on the Equestrian classification system and to Chris Meaden for offering help.

Sincere thanks to Tash Carpenter at the British Paralympic Association (BPA) for her endless patience in answering questions, perseverance and dedication in getting hold of athletes, careful fact-checking and overall professionalism. All of which was done under immense time pressure.

And my thanks to Baroness Sue Campbell and Baroness Jane Campbell for kindly providing valuable background help.

Thank you also to Tim Reddish, Chairman of the BPA for excellent background information, to Jane Jones of the BPA for help and guidance, and to Caz Walton for our various meetings and background information supplied.

I'm grateful to Ian Brittain and his excellent book, *Paralympic Games Explained*, (Routledge) who, despite pressing writing projects of his own, never failed to answer questions with clarity and kindness. The information supplied was key to the book's progression.

In the cycling community, Iga Kowalska-Owen, Communications Manager at British Cycling, did a terrific job setting up a number of key interviews and providing expert information, over many months, and delivering all with good humour and willingness.

To Martin McElhatton, Chief Executive of WheelPower, thank you for being a mine of information, for ensuring no question was too foolish to ask and for facilitating vital meetings, including spending time with Jean Stone, who shared some wonderfully touching stories which are included here.

To Tony Sainsbury, now at LOCOG, but formerly Chef de Mission for the British Paralympic Team, thank you for readily helping on a range of complex issues.

Thanks also to Caroline Searle of Matchtight in Bath for excellent recommendations and for setting up some terrific interviewees; Marshall Thomas, who provided superb information and help throughout; Stephanie Gagne, Press Officer at the Great Britain Wheelchair Basketball Association; Winnie Murphy, Marketing and Communications Manager at British Dressage; the super-efficient Hannah Hore, PR and Client Services Manager at Definitive Sports; Claire Shand, head of Communication and Marketing at the British Equestrian Federation and Katy Anderson, Senior Media Officer at UKA.

Also to Jess Whitehorn at UK Sport for guiding me through the minutiae around funding. Others who provided vital assistance include: John, Matthew, Anna and Eleanor at the RNIB, Ray Cross at the Spinal Injuries Association, Tom Dyson of British Rowing, Tim Hazell of Archery GB and Craig Spence of the International Paralympic Committee (IPC).

Considerable effort went into ensuring at least one soldier was represented here and my thanks go to Colonel David Norris (Battle

Acknowledgements

Back – Sport) for superbly pulling this off; to the Ministry of Defence for permitting it and to Major Martin Colclough for background information on the Battle Back programme.

Without the athletes there would have been no stories to tell and to all those who allowed me to interview them and for generous hospitality, thank you. In particular, the Christiansen family for opening up different avenues for me to explore and for swift, detailed information. And to Marion Aggar for a story of such dignity and integrity that continues to live with me long after the original telling. Spending time talking with Marion was one of the great privileges of this book.

My thanks also to Eva Loeffler for helping me with details about her father, Sir Ludwig Guttmann, and for the explanations of events provided.

And to Dylan Onraet of Apple White City Business Team, who had to rescue the manuscript on more than one occasion. And yes, this book was mostly written on an iPad.

All top athletes have their own trusted team alongside them and, without mine, this book would not have been possible so it belongs to all of you who have been part of it.

Thanks go to Katie and Richard for your extraordinary love, support and generosity over what seems like half a lifetime. Your heartfelt backing was integral to the successful completion of this project. And Clemmie and Hugo, thank you for endless laughter and never-ending supplies of chocolate.

Thank you, Sarah, for the enduring gift of friendship and for embodying kindness, loyalty and selflessness in all you do. To Helene and Tim for allowing me to take up near-residence while simultaneously supplying restaurant-style cuisine and for tireless, genuine offers of help. Ella and Charlie, you may never know quite how important and influential you have been!

Enormous thanks also to Andi for proving distance is no barrier to real friendship. Thank you, Eleanor and Cedric, for teaching me how to use my iPad when I should have been working and you should have been sleeping. To the irrepressible Sarah Hartley, for my daily word count and for assuring me it could be done despite my protestations.

Sandra, your guidance is extraordinary – thank you for being such a constant source of love and support.

To Sophie who encouraged me to say yes in the first place and for never doubting the final outcome.

Rosemary, thank you for helping the words to flow and for your infectious enthusiasm. Lucy, you were the catalyst for life-enhancing change and for restoring something I thought lost forever. You encouraged me to live my dreams free of fear, to never doubt them and graciously reminded me to stand in the light – the biggest gift of all.

To William and Suzue Curley and all the staff in Belgravia, thank you for delicious refreshment throughout and to Andrew, Jo, Julia and Priscilla.

I would also like to thank the incredible team at the Dame Kelly Holmes Legacy Trust and, particularly, Emma Atkins for taking such care to open a path to so many unexpected new opportunities, of which this was one.

And there is one other person without whom this particular journey might have had a very different ending – David Peterson. Despite the damage done on one particular summer's afternoon, I hope these pages prove that eventually something enormously positive emerged. This book is as much a measure of my gratitude for your work than anything else I have done. But for circumstances our paths might never have crossed. That they did was an ever-present reminder to me of how life changes in an instant.

It is long overdue – but thank you.

Finally, to Barney, my number one gold-medal-winning, top-of-the-podium fan, for making me laugh out loud every day.

Somehow, though, I doubt you will read it.

List of Acronyms

BPA: British Paralympic Association

CP: Cerebral Palsy

FISA: Fédération Internationale des Sociétés d'Aviron (International Federation of Rowing Associations)

INAS-FID: International Sports Federation for Persons with an Intellectual Disability

IOC: International Olympic Committee

IPC: International Paralympic Committee

ITTF: International Table Tennis Federation

LOCOG: London Organising Committee of the Olympic and Paralympic Games

MOD: Ministry of Defence

ParalympicsGB: British Paralympic Team at Paralympic Games. Also a brand name for the British Paralympic Association (BPA)

RDA: Riding for the Disabled Association

RNID: Royal National Institute of Blind People

SIA: Spinal Injuries Association

TeamGB: British Olympic Team at Olympic Games

Index

Index

Index

Picture Credits

The publishers would like to thank the following sources for their kind permission to reproduce the pictures in the plate section of this book.

Page 1: *(top)* S&G and Barratts/Press Association Images; (bottom) International Paralympic Committee

Page 2: *(top)* Private Collection; (bottom) International Paralympic Committee

Page 3: National Coal Board

Page 4: *(top left)* Gray Mortimore/Getty Images; (top right) Private Collection; (bottom) Tim Ockenden/Press Association Images

Page 5: *(top)* Bobby Yip/Reuters/Action Images; (bottom) Feng Li/ Getty Images

Page 6: *(top)* Elizabeth Dalziel/AP/Press Association Images; (bottom) Andrew Wong/Getty Images

Page 7: *(top)* Phil Cole/Getty Images; (left) Zhang Duo/Landov/Press Association Images; (bottom right) Jason Lee/Reuters/Action Images

Page 8: Johnny Green/Press Association Images

Every effort has been made to acknowledge correctly and contact the source and/or copyright holder of each picture and Carlton Books Limited apologises for any unintentional errors or omissions that will be corrected in future editions of this book.